Ruffled Feathers

Also by Iain Grahame

Flying Feathers

For Didy, with love

RUFFLED FEATHERS

IAIN GRAHAME

Foreword by Gerald Durrell

Illustrations by Timothy Greenwood

ST. MARTIN'S PRESS · NEW YORK

Foreword

In his previous book, *Flying Feathers*, Iain Grahame gave us a delightful account of the establishment of his bird breeding sanctuary at Daws Hall. This is the sequel to it. Now I know to my cost how difficult it is to write sequels and how seldom it is that they live up to their predecessors, but Iain Grahame has triumphed splendidly – in fact, if anything, the sequel is better than the original, a very rare occurrence.

His writing – unlike so many naturalists' writings – is pleasantly free of pomposity and he has a charming wit and a nice line in self-deprecation. Only a man who realises that he is (as we all are) a comic figure, could write with such relish of the time a gosling dropped out of his trouser-leg when he was reading the lesson in church, or recount with bashful humour the story of the amorous Paradise shelduck who fell desperately in love with him.

The book is peppered with amusing instances of this sort that invariably happen to people who keep animals but, in between, Iain Grahame gives us a lot of solid advice on the intricacies of keeping and breeding birds and on bird psychology generally. It makes fascinating reading on every level – for the person who just keeps a budgerigar, the lucky owner of a bird collection, or a person who wants to start one.

Both conservation and aviculture owe the author a debt in two ways. Firstly, his contribution to the captive breeding of rare and endangered pheasants has been spectacular; secondly, and possibly more significant, his influence in the creating of the World Pheasant Association is of great importance. The WPA has now grown into a world-wide organisation of considerable conservation value, which will help the future of many gravely endangered and beautiful birds. I know all too well the work and perseverance that has to go into the building and maintaining of such an organisation and both Iain Grahame and his hard-working, long-suffering and lovely wife are to be congratulated on their successes.

This is not an ordinary book but one to be savoured; nor is it written by an ordinary man, for what ordinary man would supply a policeman's wife with an egg to hatch out between her breasts?

Gerald Durrell

Chapter One

Man has been very aptly described 'as the mistake-making animal'. 'Homo' is a mistake-maker because he is 'sapiens' and he is 'sapiens' largely because of his mistakes. – Horace G. Hutchinson, *The Fortnightly Club*.

Many of the behavioural patterns of cats and canaries, goldfish and guinea-pigs have a common origin in all members of the animal kingdom, including ourselves. Often we tend to take their presence for granted, although the odds must be about even on whether a child's first utterance (apart from squawks and unintelligible dribbling noises) is 'Mummy', 'Daddy' or some epithet describing the household pet.

The motives of the dog, barking loudly from behind the garden fence at approaching intruders, are no different to those of its master who erected the fence. Protection of territory is as time-honoured and powerful a force as that of sex and procreation of a species. The 'pecking order' too, which is so noticeable in waterfowl, the crow family, wolves and apes, is equally prevalent among human beings. It serves several functions including the establishment of authority within any given community, the protection of the weak and the instruction of the young in the recognition of danger. Warning noises emitted by human parents to discourage children from poking their fingers into electric light sockets are identical, in both process and purpose, to those of the leader of a troop of baboons who has spotted a leopard. Any well-organized society, be it of monkeys or men, wild dogs or wolves, is ruled by one or more experienced and respected individuals, and animals at least are wise enough to know that excessive power in the hands of a hot-headed or recalcitrant minority would lead inevitably to anarchy and chaos.

Sitting, as I love to do, on one of the benches beside the ponds at our Wildfowl Farm on the borders of Suffolk and Essex, is a wonderful opportunity to study the behaviour of our own strange menagerie that we have gathered around us and to reflect on the intricacies of the varied and interwoven social patterns that emerge. Sadly, it is all too seldom that any of us gets the chance to sit and observe, for administering to the needs of upwards of a thousand assorted creatures is a time-consuming occupation.

January and February are the least hectic months on the farm, and for me they are a season of particular charm and tranquility. As the days gradually lengthen, as snowdrops give way to crocuses and the haunting scent of witch hazel fills the air, the birds sense the coming of spring. Early morning is often as numbing a time for them as it is for us. Pickaxe in one hand and bucket in the other, we progress from pen to pen, smashing the ice on the ponds and dispensing the morning feed to the waterfowl. Many of the geese and ducks will be sitting huddled together in little groups, their thick layers of feathers and down providing, even on the ice itself, warmth and protection for their feet. There is a sudden flurry of activity as we scatter their pellets on the frosty ground. Briefly stretching their stiffened limbs, they rush up for their breakfast before the sparrows and starlings, chaffinches and dunnocks, all equally ravenous, polish off what is left. Later in the day, when the ice begins to melt and the enfeebled rays of a wintry sun percolate through the branches of our huge cedar tree, there is a marked increase in activity. Pairs of ducks take to the water and, rather stiffly at first, begin to indulge in their varied displays and vocalizations. The wood ducks raise their crests and burp unashamedly; wigeon and tree ducks stretch their necks and whistle, and the shelduck set up an incessant and ear-splitting clamour. From high up in the old yews and on top of the garage roof blackbirds and thrushes break forth into considerably more melodious song. The males of these garden birds are not (as is sometimes supposed) singing for joy, and the varied noises that echo round the farm are all motivated more by the establishment and protection of territory than by *joie de vivre* or any other instinct.

Why any bird should choose to nest when the snow lies thick on the ground and the east wind cuts through to the marrow of one's bones is quite extraordinary. However, a few creatures that we keep almost invariably select this impossible time of the year to lay their first clutches of eggs. They, or rather their ancestors, originated from the southern hemisphere, but even the fact that long lines of their forbears were born north of the equator in captivity has not changed their antipodean habits. Our Australian shelduck, for instance, always lay in January or February and consequently they are not the easiest of birds to rear. Most ducks are remarkable for their stupidity when it comes to bringing up a family, and that is one reason why most of their eggs have always been consigned to broody hens or incubators. This system certainly has enabled a far larger quantity of ducklings to be reared here than by letting nature run its course and, in the particular case of Sheila and Sheldon, an 'adoption scheme' is essential. Sheila, the female Australian shelduck, is one of the most prolific layers on the farm and regularly churns out more than her own body-weight in eggs every year, but it is her selection of nesting sites that causes problems. Her favourite place for depositing her eggs is at the bottom of her pond and, when a severe frost renders this impossible, she merely parks them neatly on the ice. It is not only a severe test of Sheldon's virility, but also of our ingenuity in rescuing what to her are obviously highly distasteful objects, that we succeed in rearing any of their offspring.

I should, perhaps, at this stage, explain briefly who 'we' are. Apart from Didy and myself (whose main functions are answering the telephone, paying the bills and placating the bank manager) and Tony and his wife Jean, who lend their hands to anything from housework to unblocking the drains for four mornings a week, the whole enterprise is controlled

3

by a gargantuan Dutchman. If you can visualize a gentle, cigar-smoking Viking, who wears size sixteen gumboots and a totally inappropriate Leninist cap, you will have a fair picture of our farm manager. Cees (which is pronounced like 'case') and his wife Hedy came here early in 1967 and if during these past eleven years Daws Hall Wildfowl Farm has achieved anything at all of merit, it is almost entirely due to his herculean endeavours and unfailing good humour. While Samson, shorn of all his hair, wielded the jawbone of an ass with lethal effect and 'took the doors of the gate of the City, and the two posts, and went away with them, bar and all', Cees (with blond locks and beard intact) devotes his incredible strength to more peaceful but no less energetic pursuits. Scorning all forms of modern machinery, with the sole exception of a tiny tractor for cutting the grass, on which he perches like Goliath astride a Shetland pony, he excavates new ponds for the waterfowl with just a spade and shovel, cuts up vast trees with a hand-saw and on one occasion shifted over a hundred tons of sand into the pheasant aviaries by wheelbarrow. With that inherent determination which takes men to the tops of the highest mountains and to the depths of the ocean, he views every task on the farm as a challenge to his physical prowess. On the rare occasions that Tony or I have been rash enough to volunteer to help him in any particular labour, we have finished up laden like pack mules and crippled for weeks. The only time that I can recall him being anything less than the proverbial gentle giant was several years ago when we were taking the honey crop. One brave bee discovered a chink in his armour, and, too late, he realized that he had left his fly-buttons undone.

Even the strongest of mortals have their Achilles' heel, but in his case it is one that is rather surprising. Most of us take for granted coughs and colds, bumps and bruises and the occasional attack of hiccoughs. Cees, when afflicted by any such ailment, is convinced that the hour of doom is upon him. Fortunately for all of us these are rare events, but when they do happen the whole farm is thrown into a state of turmoil. We all have to go into premature mourning until the great moment arrives when he announces, always in a tone of naïve amazement, that his health is once more restored. Even this, however, is not always as straightforward as might be imagined, for his concern over any ailment is equalled only by his horror of what the doctor may prescribe for its treatment. Even a routine visit to the dentist for his annual check-up is a fearful and horrific event in which we all have to participate.

It was Tony who found him one morning sitting in what appeared to be indescribable pain outside the pheasant aviaries, ashen-faced and clutching his left ankle.

'Ooch, my leg, my leg,' he was wailing, 'I theenk it is very bad.'

Tony, naturally fearing the worst, rushed up to the house for help. Leaving Jean behind to telephone for the doctor, the rest of us raced to the scene of the accident. The patient had by now succeeded in dragging himself into a more comfortable position and was trying with obvious difficulty to peel off one enormous gumboot. As gentle fingers helped him guide the boot over his heel, we prepared ourselves for the shock of seeing pools of blood, or even a fractured tibia protruding through the skin. We found nothing but a size eighteen sock surrounding seemingly unblemished flesh. Unable to bear the suspense any longer, I made a grab at the sock, to which Cees responded with a great howl of pain. All our enquiries as to the circumstances of his mishap elicited nothing more than further groans of distress, punctuated by the occasional Dutch expletive.

'I vill take it off myself,' he eventually announced with remarkable stoicism, gritting his teeth for the final ordeal. Inch by inch the great woollen garment was unpeeled until at last, when it was half off his foot, he pointed to a minute pin-prick just below the ankle bone. 'My voond,' he announced with enormous solemnity.

As we gathered round to inspect the damage, Cees volunteered an explanation.

'I vas collecting the eggs in the Siamese fireback pen, und voomf! He stuck his spur right through my vellington boot.'

'Bloody 'ell,' said Tony, 'I thought you was flippin' dyin'.'

At that moment the jovial figure of our local doctor hove into sight, the stethoscope round his neck swinging from side to side as he hastened up to where we were grouped round the casualty. Cees, sensing his cue, emitted a series of deep-throated moans.

'Poor old boy, what's happened to you? Toppled off a ladder? Let's get your boot off and we'll soon see what the trouble is.'

'But I haf got my boot off,' said Cees pathetically, pointing with his great forefinger at 'ze voond'.

'Well, that's easy enough to deal with,' said the doctor, opening his black bag and producing a hypodermic syringe. 'I'll just give you an anti-tetanus jab and you'll soon be as right as rain.'

At the mention of the impending injection Cees's jaw sagged and his eyes stared in horror at the needle being inserted into a small phial of liquid. 'P-p-plees . . .!' he implored, but it was too late. As the needle entered his skin, he cast his eyes heavenwards and uttered one last moan before passing out.

Holes in Cees's 'vellingtons' were always a source of worry, since size sixteen gumboots are by no means easy to acquire. This particular hole, started by the near-lethal attack of the Siamese fireback (a pheasant that stands all of thirty centimetres high), gradually widened. To make matters worse, Cees was reluctant to repair the perforation since, having by now recovered from his ordeal, the evidence had to be proudly exhibited to every visitor to the farm. The length of the cock pheasant's spur and the nature of the appalling gash in his ankle increased every time that the drama was recounted.

It was at this time that the pump situated in the Losh-house brook, at the bottom of the farm, started to cause trouble. When it functioned properly, four or five hundred gallons of water were pumped up every hour to the duck-ponds, but now a mere dribble was trickling through to the island pond. Tony was on holiday that week, so I asked Cees to see if he could find out what the trouble was and rectify the situation. He soon discovered that the problem was a build-up of silt in the concrete tank beside the brook, through which all the water had to pass, but went on to explain that, because of his tattered 'vellington', he would need assistance from us in dredging the tank. Dutifully, we accompanied him to the site, armed with thigh boots, ropes, buckets and shovel. Cees prised open the lid of the tank and we all peered down into the murky water below. A throaty, gurgling noise from the area of the outlet pipe confirmed that his diagnosis was correct.

Having recently been subjected to a hip replacement oper-ation, I felt quite justified in declining to perform any pot-holing acrobatics. Cees and I both looked at Didy, but she had already appreciated that the call of duty had fallen on her and was busy tucking her fair hair under one of my tweed caps. Cees very chivalrously assisted in lowering her into the abyss and there was a distant splash as her thigh-boots broke the surface.

'There's at least two foot of slush in here,' she exclaimed in horror when she was finally standing on the bottom, with only my cap and the top of her head visible through the aper-ture.

Cees secured one end of the rope to the handle of a bucket and, as he lowered it into the hole, Didy had to back right against the concrete wall to allow it space to enter. Having made this valuable contribution, Cees repaired to a nearby tree-stump where he sat down and lit a cigar.

For a while nothing but shovelling noises and unladylike language emerged from the pit, and then there was a shout of 'First bucket ready for hoisting!' Cees obligingly came over to receive the consignment, but the raising of a full bucket of sludge into a position where he could grasp the rope was no simple operation. Didy was forced to go through some highly complicated and uncomfortable contortions before she was able to hand him the load. When Cees eventually succeeded in grabbing the rope, the top three inches of liquid in the bucket slurped all over her before he could ease it away from the narrow hole. The rest of the slush he emptied onto the ground. While she tried to wipe the worst of the filth off her face with the back of one muddy hand, I offered some gratuitous advice on how to keep clean in the circumstances and Cees returned to his tree-stump. After half an hour of uninterrupted labour by the only female member of the party, the whole area round the pit was ankle-deep in mud and Didy's appearance resembled that of a scrum-half at Twickenham after a torrential downpour.

Cees, surveying the scene, declared solemnly, 'Ooch, it is too vet for my vellingtons.'

'Sod your bloody wellingtons,' came the retort from the deep.

The pit was almost clear now, we were informed, and a couple more bucketfuls should complete the job. I dutifully volunteered to take receipt of these. As I was hauling out the first of these I noticed something wriggling on the top. It was a small eel. Knowing Didy's fear of snakes and similar creatures, I was thankful that she had not seen it, and refrained from making any comment. As soon as her head was lowered once more, I chucked it into the brook.

'Vy do you throw it avay?' enquired Cees. 'Een Holland ve eat eelce.'

The shovelling and slurping noises from the pit came to an abrupt halt and the tweed cap shot to the surface.

'Did you say eels?' a little voice squeaked in horror.

'Just one tiny one, darling,' I interjected quickly. 'It is probably the only one in the pit.'

As the last bucket came up towards the surface, I saw Didy peering anxiously at the contents as they passed inches away from her face.

'Quick! Grab the bucket,' she screamed. 'There are hundreds of horrible eels in it.'

Ignoring his torn boots, Cees rushed up to inspect this unexpected gastronomic bonus, showering Didy with more mud from his elephantine boots in the procees. After hoisting her out of the pit, he immediately turned his attention to the bucket.

'You have done very vell,' Cees conceded. 'Hedy and I vill have lots of lovely smoked eelce to eat.'

Apart from his terror of being struck down by some incurable complaint, or being subjected to any more of the doctor's instant remedies, Cees's other phobia is for rats and mice. The actual catching of them in fact is something in which he takes the greatest pleasure, but not so the handling of the victims. As on any farm, these rodents are a constant nuisance and, since rats are potential killers of our smaller birds, we wage a remorseless campaign against them. Any signs of fresh rat droppings or a newly tunnelled hole will galvanize Cees into instant action which continues, by use of poisons, traps and less conventional methods, until the creatures have been summarily despatched. Hordes of mice are only an indirect threat to our birds, through carrying disease, but unless controlled they are capable of causing expensive damage in the foodshed and other buildings.

We have always maintained a large flock of chickens and bantams, which we use in conjunction with incubators for hatching the eggs of ornamental waterfowl and pheasants. These old-fashioned breeds of poultry are very different to the gormless modern hybrids that churn out 'farm fresh' eggs from their horribly cramped and overcrowded abodes.

Our hundred and fifty odd silkies, old English game and North Holland blues lead a happy outdoor life and muster a daily total of about fifteen eggs between them at peak laying period. This lack of productivity, however, is amply compensated by their remarkable talents as broodies. It does not matter what month any eggs are laid, for even in the winter there will always be at least half a dozen 'cluckers' in the henhouse. April till the end of June is when they are at their busiest, and at that time of the year anything up to sixty of them will be sitting patiently on valuable clutches of eggs in the brooder-shed, which is next door to their own quarters. The correct degree of humidity is very important in hatching pheasant and waterfowl eggs and we achieve this by having the rows of broody boxes sitting on a brick-surrounded pit containing damp earth and peat. When winter comes the pit has long since dried out and becomes a popular home for armies of mice.

It is then that Cees organizes periodic rodent hunts. First, the arena is cleared for action. This entails Cees and Tony carrying the nest-boxes outside; then a long hose, which can reach to the furthest end of the pit, is fitted to the tap outside the foodshed, all the entrances are blocked up and the men arm themselves for the fray. Tony, who does not believe in using a sledgehammer to crack a nut, is quite content with a walking-stick or broom handle, but for Cees nothing less than the heaviest farm shovel or a crowbar will suffice. The tap is turned on and Tony inserts the end of the hosepipe into the first mouse-hole. When the water begins to flood into their winter homes, the wretched mice make a hasty evacuation. As they scatter in all directions, Tony quickly withdraws the hose and plays it on them as they scurry along the walls and under the incubators. Cees meanwhile is to be seen rushing from place to place in his enormous boots, shouting directions to Tony and pausing only to bring down shovel or crowbar with a sickening thud on some small and bedraggled body. As the action increases, the brooder-house begins to resemble the streets of Pamplona during the running of the bulls.

The last part of the proceedings is more like the finale to a hare shoot in Bavaria. The 'bag' is collected off the floor – Cees of course either delegating this job to Tony or else cautiously scooping them up with his shovel – and lined up in immaculate formation, like guardsmen on parade, on top of the brick wall. Tony on these occasions will be heard to remark that this final ritual is 'a waste of bleedin' time', but to Cees it is the most important event of all. There the bodies have to remain until Didy, Jean, myself and anyone else who happens to be passing have all been to inspect the trophies. As we dutifully proffer our congratulations, our attention will almost inevitably be drawn to one particular victim and we are then subjected to a graphic account from the great hunter of how it met its demise.

Cees's system of catching moles is equally unconventional but no less effective. Particularly in the damp areas around the ponds we are subjected to occasional invasions by these creatures, for which I must confess to having rather a soft spot. As with my bees, their remarkable sensory system and tremendous activity invariably fill me with admiration. Cees, however, does not share my feelings when they come into the very tidy waterfowl enclosures that he has created, and the appearance of any new molehill is immediately spotted by him. The long-handled rabbiting-spade is stuck in the ground nearby and every time that he passes that particular site, on his twice daily feeding rounds or for any other purpose, his eagle eye is on the lookout for a mole that is digging near the surface. Often I have seen him suddenly freeze in his tracks and then tiptoe (not the easiest mode of progress for him) stealthily towards the spade. Having grasped it he stands like some Grecian sculpture, poised for instant action. As soon as he sees fresh activity from the molehill, down comes the spade in a huge scooping motion. Usually the mole will go soaring into the air followed by a great cry of triumph, but occasionally nothing but a rather disconsolate and blasphemous shout of *Godverdommen!* is to be heard as the quarry eludes him.

After Sheldon's and Sheila's half-hearted attempts to breed, the next waterfowl to nest are the Carolinas, Red-crested pochard and New Zealand shelduck. I aquired my first pair of the latter (often known as Paradise shelduck) several years ago and they soon became among our favourite birds on the farm. Like Sheldon and Sheila, their close relations from Australia, they are extremely noisy birds and the males of both species are often very pugnacious, not only to other waterfowl, but to humans as well. This agression, which we find in a number of birds that we keep, is something that I never mind because it is usually a sure sign of virility. Sexual virility of course means that a high percentage of eggs are likely to be fertile and we should accordingly be able to rear a good number of strong, healthy chicks. Since our main enterprise at Daws Hall Wildfowl Farm is the breeding of rare forms of waterfowl and pheasants, a high fertility rate is obviously most important.

Paradise shelduck are among the most beautiful of waterfowl. They are strong, sturdy birds in which the male and female have such markedly different plumages that it is difficult to imagine that they belong to the same species. It is a good example of what is known as sexual dimorphism. Both birds have brightly coloured wing patterns of emerald green, white and orange, but there the similarity ceases. The female has a rich chestnut body and snow-white head, while the male's plumage, which at first glance appears to be almost entirely jet black, in fact contains a subtle blend of violet, grey and deepest green.

Our first pair of Paradise shelduck, who we christened Buster and Blondie, were given a pen of their own on one of the two streams that feed the main pond, and Cees constructed in one corner of it an artificial rabbit hole for a nesting site. All forms of shelduck should start breeding in their second or third year, and disused rabbit holes are among their favourite places for depositing their clutches of anything up to sixteen pure white eggs. Buster and Blondie were at first inseparable. Whenever we ourselves or any of the other waterfowl came too close to their enclosure, Buster would rush towards the wire netting fence and drive off the intruders from the close proximity of his territory. Although they failed to breed when they were two years old, we had every hope of having offspring from them the following year. It was that winter that I began to notice a change in their relationship. They seemed literally to drift apart until, after a

12

few days, they were always to be found standing silently on opposite banks of the stream. Hitherto there had been a constant clamour from their pen which had reverberated round the whole farm, and it was the sudden absence of this noise that was so noticeable.

Paradise shelduck

One day in February I went into their enclosure to check that Blondie's tunnel-nest was clean and ready for use, though we were all agreed that once again there seemed little likelihood of their breeding that year. As I was bending down to inspect it, Blondie came coyly up to me and then, quite suddenly, made a series of high-pitched trumpeting calls, such as had previously been reserved for her husband. Buster stood on the far bank paying no attention to her at all. I instinctively extended my hand and scratched the top of her head. It is a sensitive area in birds, and it is there that the

13

male will grasp the female when they are mating. She responded by adopting a submissive posture with her body lowered to the ground and neck extended. When I lifted my fingers from her head and returned to my task of repairing a section of the tunnel which had fallen in, she remained motionless for a brief while before standing up and preening her feathers. The following two days being Saturday and Sunday, when Cees was not working, Didy and I were in charge of the farm. That weekend it was I who fed the water-fowl, and on each occasion that I passed their pen Blondie and I repeated our little game together. On the Sunday afternoon I was sawing up a large branch that had come down in the night and was working only about twenty yards from these birds. Blondie was watching my every move and trying desperately to get over her fence to join me. It slowly began to dawn on me that Cupid's tiny dart had struck home. The poor bird had fallen head over heels in love with me. For the rest of that day I could not go into their pen without her gazing admiringly into my eyes and tugging suggestively at my trousers.

While flattered at this unexpected bestowal of her favours, I was conscious that our relationship was destined to be both embarrassing and unproductive. Somehow the unholy alliance had to be broken up and Blondie reunited with her rightful mate. It seemed only proper in the circumstances that I should first apprise my own wife of the situation. This I duly did, avowing my innocence, and when she merely laughed and said, 'Oh, ho, ho!, and who's a pretty boy?,' I took it that I had been forgiven. Cees and Tony, rather to my annoyance, also found it intensely amusing, though I believe they were both rather jealous. Cees at first suggested that I should grow a beard and Tony's idea was that I should emigrate. Since I had no particular wish to do either we racked our brains for a better solution. At that moment Didy came onto the farm to join us, and she suggested that we should introduce a second female into the pen.

'I'm sure,' she said, 'that if we do this, one or other of them

14

is going to make advances towards Buster and we can then sell the odd one out.'

It all seemed rather far-fetched and unnecessarily complicated to me, but appreciating a woman's natural instinct for coping with such situations, we agreed to give it a try. I knew of a dealer who had a surplus hen bird that was coming up for two years of age and by the following afternoon the *ménage à trois* was complete. The new female wasted no time in making advances to Buster. Spurned of all love for so long, he seemed happy to reciprocate these feelings and once again the noise of these birds echoed round the farm and garden. On my only visit to their pen during that week I noticed Blondie standing disconsolately on her own, while Buster and the new arrival were indulging in a vociferous and animated exchange of conversation.

When the weekend came and Didy and I were able to exchange our desk-bound duties for incubators and outdoor exercise, I was able to spend more time observing the Paradise shelduck. At first, during the Saturday morning feed, it struck me that they were much quieter than earlier in the week. Blondie and the new female were together on the water, eyeing each other suspiciously, and I noticed that the former always positioned herself so that she was between Buster and 'the other woman'. Much to my relief, she made no advances whatsoever towards me. By the following day the young female was quite definitely the odd one out and any attempt by her to seduce Buster was instantly greeted with a hostile reaction from Blondie. When I myself climbed into the pen and approached the pair, she had no hesitation in diverting her aggression towards me while loudly inciting Buster to show his mettle. He promptly rushed up and, seizing my stockinged leg, proceeded to belabour me heftily with his wings. A new home was found for the young female and within six weeks there was a complete clutch of eggs in Cees's artificial rabbit hole. When these were removed and given to one of the larger matrons in the hen-house, the shelduck nested again and this time we left the parent birds to bring off and rear their own young.

Didy's brainwave had provided a happy outcome to their complicated love life. But it is not always that we have been able to find a cure for such psychological and emotional problems as occasionally afflict members of our menagerie. Sadly, such situations are by no means unique among captive birds and animals and are directly attributable to the unnatural environment in which they are kept. The greater the number of successive generations born in captivity, the higher the incidence of such uncharacteristic behaviour. Imprinting by goslings and (to a lesser degree) ducklings on the humans who rear them can be readily induced, while lesbianism, homosexuality and sex changes also occur from time to time.

Like many owners of zoos, wildlife parks and private collections, we believe that no joy can match that of seeing rare and beautiful creatures in their natural habitat. However, due to the ever-increasing pressures exerted on wildlife and wild places by the human race, every single year makes this ideal less feasible. Even in the fourteen years since Daws Hall Wildfowl Farm was established, the wild status of many species of waterfowl and pheasants that we keep has undergone marked changes. Habitat destruction, civil disorders, pollution and other factors have combined to make it increasingly important for viable breeding populations to be established in safer areas and under proper management to ensure the preservation of many endangered forms of wildlife.

The actual manner of keeping such species is something which has always worried us, and it is now generally accepted that much research is still needed on this subject. The days when zoos were merely required to exhibit a few camels and Indian elephants for children to ride on and a variety of strange and exotic mammals, birds and reptiles for the general amusement of *homo sapiens* are now, thankfully, over.

In many countries a growing awareness of the problem is

beginning to be manifested and the general public is becoming increasingly more critical of the conditions in which wild animals are kept and exhibited.

At our own farm we have devoted much time and thought to what are the optimum captive conditions for the birds that we keep. Since we never allow visitors during the breeding season we naturally avoid some of the problems inherent to many zoos. Nevertheless, without unlimited financial resources, it is still no easy matter, for the natural homes of our birds vary from the snow-clad peaks of the Himalayas to the tropical and sub-tropical jungles and waterways of Malaysia, Indo-China and Africa.

Apart from several common and indigenous species, our waterfowl are pinioned and kept within the confines of an eight foot high perimeter fence. If they were not, they would soon either populate the surrounding countryside or else fall prey to foxes and other vermin. A plentiful supply of natural water runs through the various ponds that we have constructed and there is ample cover for the birds to breed.

Our pheasants are given the freedom of their wings, but only in a restricted fashion, since we keep them in covered aviaries. These aviaries we endeavour to make as clean and attractive as possible by having sparrow-proof wire netting, a floor of washed sand and judicious planting of suitable trees and shrubs. Pheasants that would otherwise be unable to withstand the rigours of our English climate are supplied with specially heated winter quarters.

Every year we make mistakes and every year we carry out new experiments in aviary design, nutrition, disease control, behaviour and so on. Others with considerably more scientific expertise are making a far greater contribution towards the conservation of these birds, but the importance of proper standards of captive management is now generally accepted. In this respect we believe that the observations of the 'backyard' breeder, particularly if he specializes in just a few rare or endangered species, can often be just as valuable as those by the overworked staffs of laboratories or large zoos.

Pooling of resources and research findings is a fundamental necessity in preserving many threatened forms of wildlife for posterity. All of us, however, as Konrad Lorenz wisely councels, must avoid the pitfall of 'confounding information with knowledge'.[1]

[1] *Studies in Animal and Human Behaviour*, Vol. 1 (Methuen & Co. Ltd.)

Chapter Two

'Bare Winter suddenly was changed to Spring' – Shelley,
The Question.

By the middle of April the first chicks are strong enough to be
transferred to their outdoor rearing quarters, and every day
an increasingly varied selection of eggs is collected from the
aviaries and waterfowl enclosures and taken down to the
cellar in the house. There they are stored, at the correct temperature, until such time as we consign them to incubators or
broody hens for hatching. This we try to do within a week of
their being laid, although it is perfectly possible to store eggs
for as long as three weeks and still get strong, healthy chicks.

The bees have for several weeks been hard at work in the
garden and from now until the end of the summer weekly
visits have to be made to the hives; queen cells need to be
pinched out and extra space provided for the growing
broods and influx of honey. This is one job that is entirely
my responsibility. Cees used to help me with the bees until
that memorable day when a bee invaded his trousers.
Nothing will now induce him to venture anywhere near the
hives.

At this time of the year the waterfowl cause us comparatively few problems. There are some ducks admittedly, who
just drop their eggs in the open for any visiting magpie or
crow to steal, while others hide their nests with such cun-
ning that the finding of them takes us days of searching, but
the large majority use the various boxes, barrels and tunnels
which we supply for this purpose. Our swans and geese
guard their nests so fiercely that the location and protection

of these is never cause for any anxiety. The pheasants, however, invariably give us plenty of headaches when spring is in the air. Many of the cock birds are not content with the conventional methods of reproduction and resort to wife-battering, egg-eating and a variety of other perversions. In the early days on the farm, before we had designed proper protective measures for the females, it was not unusual to find a hen bird resembling the victim of a Red Indian scalping. Even if we succeeded in saving her life by stitching together the tattered shreds of skin on her head, she would be of no further use for the remainder of that breeding season.

One of the birds most prone to these vicious assaults is the monal pheasant, a large and beautifully coloured species in which the head, neck and back of the male are a vivid, metallic blend of violet, green and burnished gold. Its strong, curved beak not only enables it to dig through thick layers of snow for bulbs and roots in the high Himalayas, but also serves as a lethal weapon for wife-battering. A female monal is one pheasant which one has little chance of saving once such a murderous assault has been launched. We had one old male, whom we christened Jaws, who had already succeeded in slaughtering one bride, and the following year we were determined that no such fate should befall her successor. Cees and I caught him up in the trout landing-net, ·which we used whenever we wanted to handle a bird, and we then proceeded to reduce his natural armoury. With a strong pair of nail clippers we trimmed his upper mandible and spurs and then cut back the primary feathers on one of his wings. Old Christmas trees and piles of brushwood were placed at the back of their covered shelter and we felt we had done everything possible for her protection. Thereafter, on most occasions that we passed their pen she was to be seen sitting safely on the high perch, while Jaws, unable to reach her, was venting his wrath on the sand below, hacking at it with his foreshortened but still formidable bill. There was a large juniper bush growing in the middle of the aviary and every time that we fed them we were careful to throw some of

20

the corn, pellets or fruit on each side of this so that she could alight and feed unharmed.

One afternoon in late April, I had just dispensed their ration to the monals and was carrying on down the line of pheasant aviaries when I suddenly heard a shriek. Looking up, I was just in time to see the female fly at full speed from the back of their long aviary towards the front. As she hit the wire-netting it parted like the waters of the Red Sea and, sailing majestically over the oak trees, she landed a good three hundred yards away in our neighbour's winter wheat. Jaws stood, furious and frustrated, with a mouthful of feathers in his beak. As I was carrying out makeshift repairs to the fencing and wondering how on earth one set about catching a free-winged pheasant in the middle of a forty acre field, Didy came up from feeding the waterfowl at the bottom end of the farm. I told her what had happened. Ever optimistic, she volunteered to go off and try to catch it.

'I think your only chance,' I said, 'is to go right round behind the bird and try and walk her back slowly in this direction. If you can get her near the perimeter fence, give me a shout and I'll bring the net.'

As I continued feeding the chickens and the rest of the pheasants, I was thinking that the only consolation was that the poor bird had at least been saved from mutilation by her husband and would be able to lead a happy life in the wild. The possibility that Didy *might* get within twenty yards of it before it took to its wings once more was inconceivable. Having collected the chicken eggs and closed up the foodshed, I strolled over towards the big cedar beside the main pond from where there was a good view across our neighbour's field. Didy had done as I suggested and I saw her walking very, very slowly towards the pheasant, which was still sitting where it had landed. She was about forty yards from the bird and I calculated that she had somehow to move it another two hundred yards in my direction before there was any hope of our netting it. Five minutes later the gap had been shortened to the length of a cricket pitch and

21

any moment I expected to see the monal take to its wings. Sure enough, this was exactly what happened, but surprisingly the bird only flew a very short way before realighting once more in the field.

Didy again set off stealthily towards it. Her progress was tantalizingly slow, and I could not but give her full marks for patience and determination. Another five minutes went by and, incredibly, there was now only five or six yards between them. I wished I had given her the net, since at that range there was just an outside chance that she might have caught it. For several moments she stood quite motionless and I held my breath in expectation. Then, inch by inch, she began to ease herself forward again. When she was no more than a yard away she suddenly launched herself into a flying tackle and landed spread-eagled among the young shoots of corn. I had a momentary vision of it being completely flattened by this onslaught, and I could see Didy fumbling under her bosom. At last, she picked herself off the ground and held the fit and flapping escapee aloft in triumph.

It took Cees a long time to realize that Didy was not pulling his leg when she recounted the incident to him the following morning. It was not the only occasion that free-winged pheasants have escaped from their aviaries and though all of them have been recaptured, usually by Cees's adroit handling of the trout net, Didy's remarkable feat with Jaws's bride is unlikely ever to be surpassed.

It was not long after this that a male Malay peacock pheasant got out. This particular escape was made possible by the collusion of a couple of delightfully tame Emperor goslings that we had reared without the assistance of a broody and which had accepted us as their parents. They normally stayed around the foodshed, grazing the grass in this area and rushing up to greet us whenever we came onto the farm. They were an inquisitive and meddlesome pair and were at their happiest when tampering with the rotary grass-cutter or undoing people's shoelaces. The peacock pheasant aviaries are opposite the foodshed and it must have been our two busybodies who had fiddled with the hook-and-eye fastener of one of these doors. Our first intimation of the escape was when Cees found the door open and, looking up, saw the cock bird sitting happily at the top of a large sycamore tree. The hen, fortunately, had been slow to take advantage of this opportunity and was still inside the aviary. It was a particularly serious catastrophe, for at that time they were the only pair of Malay peacock pheasants in captivity in the whole country. To make matters even worse, the escaped cock did not even belong to us, but was on loan from the New York Bronx Zoo. It had been a difficult task to persuade the Director that we and our small establishment were fit custodians for this extremely rare bird, and I shuddered to think what his reaction would be when he heard of our neglect.

How we were to recapture the bird was quite beyond me. I knew that the Fire Brigade were called out occasionally to rescue maniacs who threatened to throw themselves down from cliff tops and church steeples, but I could not see them being amused by an invitation to rescue a small pheasant from the top of a tree. Just as we were looking helplessly at the tiny speck that was only just visible through the branches I heard the crunch of gravel on the drive. It was Didy returning from the railway station with a notable pheasant breeder from Spain, who had come over to this country to see our collection of birds. By a strange and unfortunate coincidence, he was a personal friend of the Director of the Bronx Zoo. Leaving Cees and Tony with a despairing valediction of, 'For Christ's sake do your best but don't tell Manuel what's happened,' I went off to greet our guest.

Didy, he and I set off on our tour of inspection of the farm, and, after some frantic whispering with Didy, I was able to explain to him that it would be more convenient if we looked at the waterfowl first and left the pheasants till last. As we steered him through the back gate towards the main pond I glanced quickly behind me and could see Tony half way up the sycamore and Cees hurling sticks and stones into the upper regions of the tree. At that moment the peacock pheasant gave its unmistakable alarm call and flew in our direction, this time settling much lower down in one of the weeping willows. The Spaniard fortunately had noticed nothing, but it was clear that he was not very interested in the waterfowl.

'I am looking forward so much to seeing your pheasants,' he kept saying, while looking with little enthusiasm at the various ducks and geese disporting themselves on the pond, and then, a little later, 'I hear you have the very rare Malay peacock pheasant in your collection.'

'Um, ah, yes,' I replied, glancing surreptitiously towards that willow tree, where the bird appeared poised for instant flight into the surrounding countryside. 'The, er, male has actually been a bit off colour for a few days and the farm manager may be taking it down to the vet this morning.'

As we proceeded down to the island pond and bottom pond, a muted *Godverdommen* from Cees floated down on the breeze, but this time I dared not look backwards. After Didy had given a lengthy and eulogistic commentary on the display of the European goldeneye and I had stopped twice to shake non-existent stones out of my gumboots, we eventually turned round and headed in the direction of the pheasant aviaries. The Spaniard quickened his step and I noticed that there was an ominous silence from the area of the weeping willow. Passing briefly by the pens of blood pheasant, argus and other rarities, we continued towards the range of aviaries that house the various species of peacock pheasant that we keep. It was while our guest was admiring the beautiful display of the comparatively common 'Chinquis', (or grey peacock pheasant) that Cees and Tony emerged, grinning happily, from the wood behind us. Clutched in Cees's huge hands was the valuable property of the Bronx Zoo, while Tony was carrying the long aluminium extension handle for the pruning saw which we use in the poplar plantations. In the hollow top section of this was the trout landing net. With an ill-disguised sigh of relief I signalled them to walk out of view behind the foodshed with their respective burdens. By the time we got to the Malay peacock pheasant aviary, Tony was singing *Sparrow in the Tree Tops*, while tipping corn into the food-bins, and Cees, watched by the Emperor goslings, was occupied in moving the hook-and-eye fastener to a position on the door that was out of their reach. Manuel stood regarding the two rare pheasants with obvious pleasure. I introduced Cees and the corduroy Leninist cap was doffed as they shook hands.

'Oh, but they are wonderful!' he exclaimed. And then, after a pause: 'The cock bird looks remarkably fit to me.'

Cees and I exchanged glances. 'I theenk he is much better now than he vas ven you arrived,' he said while gazing inscrutably in the direction of the weeping willow.

Although we would never consider releasing peacock pheasants intentionally, there are certain pheasants that we do allow to run at liberty on the wildfowl farm within the confines of the eight foot high perimeter fence. Golden pheasants, the first species that I ever acquired, were given the run of the whole wood round the main pond and lived and bred there very happily for a number of years. Blue and white peafowl (which are also members of the pheasant family) have also alternated between the farm and French windows leading into the kitchen, where they used to come for their daily ration of cheese. After a time, however, their bad gardening habits and strident calls forced us to dispense with their company. Sometimes we rear young pheasants which have twisted toes or other deformities, thus rendering them useless for stock or sale. Rather than wring their necks, these birds are lightly feather-clipped and released into the wood, where the majority stay and lead a happy existence. The various forms of eared pheasants (or Crossoptilons) are large birds that by nature very seldom take to their wings and on one occasion we intentionally released a small flock of brown eared pheasants. These birds are officially listed as endangered and very little is known about their current status in their native China. That they are rare in the wild and horribly inbred in captivity is certain. Most if not all captive stock is descended from five birds imported in the 1860s. The joy of being able to keep them outside the confines of an aviary and of watching them calling loudly to each other on a summer's evening as they hopped up to roost in the oak trees was, however, short lived. One day after they had been busy digging with their powerful beaks in an area that was once an old rubbish dump, Cees and I found two of them suffering from the awful, paralyzing symptoms of lockjaw, or tetanus. They expired in terrible agony in our hands.

Waterfowl, by and large, are easier to keep at liberty than pheasants and, if left unpinioned where they are born, there is a good chance that they will not stray far. I personally get as much pleasure from watching our own small flock of free-winged barnacle geese as I do from all the other waterfowl put together, but for reasons of safety I would never advocate the keeping of any but the commoner species in this way.

To return to the Crossoptilons. We were fortunate enough to acquire in 1972 a pair of the extremely rare white eared pheasants from Jersey Zoo. This species, which is also listed as endangered, originates from China as well. Although a few specimens of this magnificent bird – the Polar bear of the pheasant family – had been sent to various zoos throughout the world since the 1890s, it was not until shortly before the last world war that the species was first bred in captivity. ·Two American-born Chinese brothers who were leading an expedition into Tibet to obtain the giant panda and certain rare relics of ancient history for Theodore and Kermit Roosevelt, agreed to try to collect live specimens of this pheasant for a breeder in California. Although they found the white eared pheasant to be relatively tame and common at altitudes of around 11,000 feet, the problems of transporting trapped birds overland to Shanghai, a journey of three thousand odd miles, and thence by sea to California were immense. In 1935 the first two live white eared pheasants arrived in America. Unfortunately, both turned out to be cocks.

The following year one of the brothers was persuaded to

The white eared pheasant, an inhabitant of high Tibetan mountain ranges

return to Tibet. After trapping thirty Crossoptilons, he sent these coastwards in bamboo wicker baskets carried by coolies, while he himself went back with the rest of his party to collect some more. The entire first consignment was eaten by Communist bandits and the same fate very nearly befell the second lot of thirty. Eventually, after a long and arduous journey involving crossing precipitous mountain passes and travelling by raft down the Yangtze River, nineteen birds arrived at Shanghai. There, the ubiquitous customs officials subjected these birds to their own special brand of oriental scrutiny and delayed their shipment still further. The nine birds that finally reached San Francisco were more dead than alive and soon only four remained. There was just one solitary hen among them. The following spring, in 1938, this female laid and four offspring were successfully reared. In spite of this encouraging start, the captive population of these creatures of the high Tibetan mountains gradually dwindled. By 1966 there was not a single viable breeding group in captivity anywhere in the world outside China.

Gerald Durrell's account[1] of how the Jersey Wildlife Preservation Trust succeeded in importing four birds in the summer of that year and breeding from them in the Channel Islands is well known. At the time of writing, one of the original pairs still survives and their progeny are distributed among zoos and other collections throughout the world.

Our own pair was born in Jersey in 1972 and Cees flew over from London Airport to collect them when they were about six months old. The Curator of Birds at Jersey is not only a friend of ours, he is a man who, like us, believes in pandering to the needs of his birds. A large wooden crate with padded roof had been constructed for the shipment of our pair and it was with this that Cees duly boarded the aeroplane for his flight back to London that afternoon. Having cleared them through customs, his next task was to get them to Liverpool Street Station and thence by rail to Colchester, where his car was waiting. Had I been in his position, some

---

[1] *Catch me a Colobus*, Gerald Durrell, (Collins, 1972).

London taxi driver would have had a lucrative trip and the birds and I would have travelled in comfort. For Cees, however, no challenge is to be ignored and, in this instance, the challenge involved his transporting them first on a double-decker bus and then on the tube during the peak rush-hour period. Despite the objections of inquisitive underground officials and irate bowler-hatted commuters, he and his precious cargo successfully traversed the capital unscathed. Whether the same could be said of his fellow-passengers, history does not relate.

On their arrival at Daws Hall the birds were installed in a well-planted and roomy aviary and soon settled happily into their new environment. Part of their staple diet in the mountainous regions of Tibet and China is allium bulbs, for which, like monal pheasants, they dig with their powerful beaks. Our pair relished onions and a variety of other vegetables, and we also periodically sowed oats a few inches under the surface of the sand. When these started to sprout, the birds got extra exercise and nutrition. They soon became great favourites of Angus, Katrina and Hugh, our three children, who were continually raiding the vegetable rack in the kitchen during school holidays for the purpose of augmenting the pheasants' diet. When the birds were two years old the female started to lay and there was great excitement on the farm when we saw her making a nesting scrape under a big laurel bush in their aviary. The first egg (as sometimes happens) was no bigger than a blackbird's, the second was promptly eaten by the cock, and the third one proved to be infertile. That was their total contribution that year, and the following year, for some strange reason the hen failed to lay at all.

It was, I recall, at this time that two of the children were, inadvertently, conducting their own nutritional trials with the birds.

We have always made a point of putting peanuts, bacon rind and so on on the bird table during the winter, and various garden birds, including four forms of titmice regularly come there to feed during the cold weather. Katrina and Hugh, who were then aged seven and six, decided that even on warm spring days these grossly overfed friends of ours required extra sustenance. A foray into the store-cupboard disclosed a tin of what they took to be roasted pea-nuts. These they duly inserted into the wire baskets hanging from the bird table, with a liberal application of further handfuls all over the lawn for good measure. They were coffee beans!

The brown eared pheasant, one of the rarest of the species in the world

It was not only with the white eared pheasants that Cees experienced difficulties on public transport. Our normal method of despatching birds to our customers in the British Isles is to put them in strong cardboard boxes, which we obtain from the local wine merchant, and in these they travel swiftly and safely by rail. A few years ago an industrial dispute affecting certain sections of British Rail resulted in a ban on their handling of livestock in some regions of the country. This ban, occurring at a time of the year when we had a very large quantity of young waterfowl, pheasants and poultry that had been ordered, was thoroughly inconvenient. A month or more went by, the food bill and my overdraft soared to astronomic heights and it was clearly time for drastic action. We made certain enquiries, from which it transpired that, if we could deliver the birds to the various main railway terminals in London, they would be duly despatched to their destinations. Hiring a van for this purpose was hardly economical, so Cees volunteered to accompany them in the passenger compartment of a train and then distribute them to the terminals by taxi. The only way this appeared feasible was for him to catch the milk train which left Colchester at about five o'clock in the morning.

It was still dark when two cars, laden to the roof with a total of twenty-three boxes, drove out from the farm. Cees, at the wheel of one, had discarded his gumboots for hand-made Dutch clogs for this rare visit to the metropolis, while I had merely thrown an overcoat over my pyjamas. While the booking clerk at the station was rubbing his hand sleepily over his eyes and issuing Cees with his return ticket, I was stealthily carrying the boxes onto the platform. When the empty train drew into the station, there were no other passengers nor railway staff in sight and Cees and his cargo just managed to squeeze into one complete passenger compartment. Wishing him luck, I returned to my bed.

It was mid-afternoon before I heard him drive up to the house.

'Ooch, vat a journey!' he announced, as he dragged his huge frame wearily out of the car.

Over a cup of tea he recounted how all had gone well as far as Shenfield, but there an announcement came over the loud-hailer that, owing to a fault on the line, London-bound

passengers had to transfer to another train. By the time Cees
had made four separate journeys with his 'luggage' to a different platform, that train had left. There was half an hour
before the next one was due and a steady stream of busi-
nessmen with their briefcases and copies of the *Financial
Times* started to congregate on the platform. Sensing trouble,
most of them gave him a wide berth. The train drew up and
Cees quickly advanced to open the nearest carriage door. He
tried to turn the knob but it just would not budge. Flexing his
muscles, he gave it a great wrench and it promptly came off
in his hand. *'Godverdommen!'* he shouted, angrily throwing it
between the lines.

A porter, hearing the commotion rushed up and explained
that he could not possibly be allowed to take twenty-three
pieces of luggage into a passenger compartment and that
they would have to be consigned to the guard's van. At that
moment one of the cockerels, aware that dawn had broken,
began to crow.

'Cor, Lofty, what yer got in them there boxes?' the porter
enquired, regarding the consignment with grave suspicion.

Realizing that the game was up, Cees confessed to the contents.

'Livestock ain't allowed on Eastern region trains,' announced the porter. 'Yor'll have to take 'em 'ome.'

'But how can I get them home, ven I am not allowed to put
them on a train?' Cees enquired pathetically.

The porter, unable to answer this one, went off in search of
the station master. Cees, stranded on the platform, now had
a further problem. Promptly at seven o'clock every morning
it is his custom to partake of a colossal breakfast and if, for
any reason, this is delayed for more than a few minutes, he
apparently experiences such severe sensations in his sto-
mach as convince him that death by starvation is imminent.
Before leaving home, he had calculated that he would be able
to indulge in this meal in London, but now his whole gastronomic programme was upset.

The station master soon arrived on the scene. For a

moment or two he stood totally dumbfounded by the strange apparition that confronted him. Bearded giants with assorted arrays of vociferous gin boxes were not among his normal clientele. He asked where Cees came from.

'Ooch, many, many miles avay,' Cees replied, pointing with one hand in the vague direction of Scotland, while with the other he endeavoured to ease the pains of hunger in his belly.

It turned out to be the trump card. The station master reluctantly agreed to allow Cees and his twenty-three boxes to continue by the next train to London, the only proviso being that the birds travel in the guard's van. It was past nine o'clock before the birds were delivered and he was finally able to have his breakfast.

Nutritional problems at Daws Hall are not just confined to the farm manager however. While Hedy; his Dutch wife, struggles bravely to provide punctual and plentiful meals for Cees, all of us are continually giving thought to improved diets for the birds. Through the development of manufactured, compound foodstuffs it is reasonably simple to keep them alive, but the successful breeding of rare creatures in captivity depends on a number of factors. Not only must the quantity, palatability and components of their food be correct, but the environment too must be to their liking. These are subjects on which zoologists, veterinarians, biochemists and others are continually working and much more research is still required. Even with our own very limited menagerie there are no straightforward solutions. Each year we succeed in gleaning a little extra knowledge, while at the same time we realize how much more we still have to learn.

While the correct combination of cereals and pelleted foodstuffs will produce a balanced proportion of protein, vitamins, minerals and trace elements suitable for poultry and (for want of a better word) the 'straightforward' breeds, other species require much more specialized treatment. This we endeavour to provide through a mixture of observation, advice from experts and various experiments.

33

During the breeding season some of our waterfowl are given dog biscuits and trout pellets. Both are high in protein and, since they float on the water, there is no loss to sparrows and other scavengers. The goldeneye and eiders, both of which live primarily on animal foods in the wild, relish this rich diet. Another source of high protein is egg and this we give to many of the pheasants in the spring. We have discovered that by hard-boiling surplus chicken eggs (or any other eggs that prove to be infertile during the hatching season) and then pushing them through the electric mincer in the kitchen, they can be presented in the ideal form. (If we were to throw whole eggs into their pens, it would merely encourage the birds to eat their own eggs.) The preparation of this particular *bonne bouche* is Didy's responsibility and about once a week from March to May Cees or I bring her an assortment of eggs from the farm. On the whole, the process works well, but it must be admitted that there have been one or two notable and noisy exceptions. On such occasions the first intimation of trouble has been what sounds like bursts of automatic rifle fire, followed by the scraping of scrambled egg off the kitchen ceiling and the purchase of one or more new saucepans.

With certain birds the problem is to keep the protein level low rather than high at the critical breeding period, and one such example is the Emperor. This medium-sized goose, with a white head and silvery-grey body breeds on the northwest coast of Alaska and around the Bering Strait. When the skeins reach this forbidding area in May and early June they immediately start to nest in the tundra. The various grasses and sedges there are still weak in nutritional value and remain so until the goslings hatch. Another bird that breeds in the far north is the red-breasted goose, considered by many to be the most beautiful goose of all. To aviculturists they are like mink coats, diamonds and heated swimming pools, all lumped together, and the acquisition of them is further complicated by the fact that only a small percentage ever breed outside their natural environment. Although this goose was kept in captivity as early as 1853, there was no breeding among captive stock for more than seventy years. In western Siberia, where these birds migrate from south of the Caspian and Aral Seas, the hours of daylight are of extremely short duration and it is significant that in the British Isles they appear to breed more frequently in Scotland than in the south of England. One year we experimented by floodlighting a solitary pair in a small enclosure close to the electricity supply in the house. The hours of darkness were reduced to those that the birds experience in the wild and this resulted in the first breeding of these tame and enchanting geese at Daws Hall.

A creature that has posed the most demanding problems to aviculturists is the blood pheasant, a small, partridge-like bird from the mountainous areas of Nepal, Bhutan, Sikkim and China. Until very recently they appeared quite impossible to keep, let alone breed, outside their natural habitat. As recently as two years ago, only three establishments had ever succeeded in propagating them in captivity outside the Orient. We were fortunate to be included in this august trio and the owners of the others – one American, one French – were close friends of ours. Needless to say, there was a good deal of friendly rivalry as each of us sought the vital clues to their management. Appreciating their grazing habits, the Frenchman kept them in aviaries where the open flights were planted with short grass. We and the Americans believed that this was courting disaster from various soil-borne diseases to which the birds are extremely susceptible. One of the American syndicate believed that altitude was the key to their success. His birds were accordingly installed on his roof-top. Both the Americans and ourselves considered that, to obviate the disease risk, clean green food and fruit should be brought to them. We experimented with various systems – lawn mowings, alfalfa (or lucerne), diced apples, rabbit pellets and so on – with only limited success. Then, one of our American friends, who had had a good breeding season with his birds, came to stay with us. As we took him and his wife on an inspection of the farm the conversation soon turned to blood pheasants. For a while we discussed the pros and cons of relative protein levels, antibiotics and the design and positioning of artificial nest-boxes.

'Well, Charlie,' I said, after a few minutes, 'I'm sure the most important thing of all is food. What do you give yours?'

He enumerated, one by one, the various ingredients that he was using. Mentally, we ticked each one off and it seemed that the diet we were offering our respective birds was identical, until the final item on his menu – fruit cocktail.

'Good heavens, Charlie! What's that?' Didy exclaimed in astonishment. 'A cross between a Pimm's and a Manhattan?'

Charlie patiently explained that there was nothing alcoholic, nothing aphrodisiacal, about this particular item, which in this country we normally know as fruit salad. Anyway, call it what you will, the same thoughts flashed through Didy's mind and my own. Were white grapes and pineapple cubes the missing links for which we had so long been searching? Do diced peaches, swimming in their syrupy juice, have some special property that was hitherto not been catalogued? Never one to falter when the moment of truth is at hand, Didy tore down to the village shop and spent half her monthly housekeeping allowance on every variety of fruit salad in stock. And the birds? They promptly suffered from an acute attack of diarrhoea and the experiment was not repeated.

Although a correctly regulated diet is certainly an important factor in the captive management of all members of the animal kingdom, it will only produce the required results if other conditions are to their liking. Proper studies on the behaviour of different species in their natural environment are essential for simulating, as far as is possible, such conditions in captivity. All too often one sees, caged up together in zoos and elsewhere, pairs of mammals, reptiles, fishes or birds, and our neat, romantic and monogamous minds assume that 'a happy event' is imminent. Some creatures, admittedly, may breed out of sheer boredom, while others who naturally pair for life are only too happy to wake up each morning and find the same face on pillow or perch. Many, however, find these enforced relationships both unpalatable and unnatural, and react strongly against them. Analogies among *homo sapiens*, where instinctive behaviour is often in direct conflict with religious and other socially imposed restrictions, are all too obvious.

Waterfowl, on the whole, adapt well to captivity. Even depriving them of their powers of flight appears to have little, if any, effect on their breeding. Since few of them are aggressive by nature, it is common practice to enclose a variety of ducks and geese together. In this way there is plenty of healthy competition. Monogamous species suffer little disturbance and the flirts and philanderers have a happy time. Pheasants, as I have already explained, have to be kept in separate aviaries, as the males of some species are notoriously aggressive towards their wives.

This poses the question: how often does wife battering occur among pheasants in the wild? The answer, so far as we know, is never. Most hen pheasants, in their natural state, expect to be taken by force. Even with the eared pheasants, in which loose flocking is common for most of the year and where the male's display is unostentatious by pheasant standards, the male must always be dominant. This is not to imply that rape by the cock bird (as is commonly seen with Muscovies) is naturally practised, for in the wild the partners will only mate when there is synchronization of reproductive cycles and after displays of courtship and submission by respective sexes. Male displays in some cases are not confined to immediately pre-copulatory periods, and anyone acquainted with the golden pheasant will have seen how the male bird will dance round his drab little wife at almost any time of the year. If the necessary synchronization, which is influenced by diet, temperature, light and other factors, is missing, there can be no successful mating. With some gamebirds, for example black grouse and American ruffed

37

grouse, the only time the sexes meet are during courtship and copulation. Instances of unnatural aggression, egg-eating, female dominance and so on are all examples of abnormal behaviour which simply do not occur under natural conditions.

Our blue eared pheasants were a typical example. Although we had bred this Chinese bird on many occasions in the past, we were anxious to establish a new and unrelated breeding trio. Accordingly, one spring, we penned up a couple of one year old Daws Hall ladies with a fine male bird from further afield who was old enough to be their father. Both our maidens were totally infatuated with this handsome Lothario and, though one does not normally expect them to breed in their first year, a large number of chicks were successfully reared. We all agreed that this trio had tremendous breeding potential. We were wrong or, to be more precise, we failed properly to appreciate their relationship and requirements.

During the course of that winter and early the following year, the two females, advancing from adolescence to mature womanhood, were acquiring minds of their own. No longer bobby-soxers, flattered by the advances of an older male, they ganged up against their erstwhile sugar-daddy and pushed him around their aviary, plucking his beautiful tail feathers and subjecting him to other indignities. Hen-pecked and submissive, he was unable to escape this unnatural avian regime of women's lib. In the wild, he would have moved off under such circumstances and only rejoined these two hussies when spring and the mating instinct returned. The previous year we had, quite fortuitously, chosen just the right seasonal and psychological moment for putting them together.

Then the two females started squabbling. Nature's main safety-valve in instances of intra-specific aggression is for the weaker opponent to capitulate before any serious damage is inflicted. Once the necessary submissive gestures have been made, honour is satisfied and the victor will not, unless

38

further provoked, administer the *coup de grâce*. We were faced, therefore, with a totally artificial situation of a timid and submissive cock bird, a submissive hen and one dominant hen who was exhibiting male demonstrative behaviour towards her companions. In mid-April both females started to lay but, not surprisingly, all the eggs in their first clutches were infertile. It was a situation of our own making and somehow we had to undo the damage that we had caused.

There was one obvious course of action that we could have taken, if we had had spare aviaries at the time. By penning each bird separately, the cock bird in his new environment would, even as sole occupant, have gradually established a degree of territorial ownership. When this had been attained, the females could, one at a time, have been frog-marched along to his kingdom and Cees would most likely have been able to report that the cock had 'done a woomf' at her. As it was, there were no empty aviaries, the laying season was only going to last for a short while and so something more drastic had to be tried. Cees and I held a brief consultation.

'I theenk,' he announced, puffing thoughtfully on his pipe, 'that we should send for Eric.'

Like many of his colleagues in the veterinary profession, Eric runs an efficient rural practice, deriving his bread and butter from the treatment of farm animals, dogs and cats. From time to time constipated hamsters, pregnant guinea-pigs and egg-bound canaries are brought into his surgery and there are periodic summonses to see other strange creatures, including our own. Together we went to the aviary containing the unharmonious *ménage à trois*. As I opened their door, the wattles of the dominant female became red and dilated with anger and she made a vicious stab at my gumboots with her beak. Her two companions slunk off furtively into the furthest corner.

'Well,' I asked the vet, 'have you got anything in your kitbag to sort out this little trio?'

'I've got just the thing to give the cock bird,' he replied.

39

'But there is one problem.'

'What's that?'

'It would probably kill the poor bugger. We give hormone injections to bulls, rams and boars, but I doubt if anyone has ever tried it out on a cock pheasant.'

Anxious to avoid the farm manager's opprobrium if the bird were to drop down dead at our feet, I shouted for Cees. Having explained our dilemma, I asked, 'What do you think? Shall we give it a go?'

'I theenk it best that ve give him a leetle dose now, und then, eef all goes vell, he can have a bigger dose next veek.'

Eric agreed that this seemed a sensible arrangement, so the cock was duly caught up and injected. As the needle was withdrawn and the bird put gently down on the ground we all held our breath. Quite unconcernedly, however, he trotted back to his shelter, jumped up onto the perch and appeared to be none the worse for his experience.

Even with this small dose the effect on his behaviour was quite remarkable, and, within twenty-four hours of the second injection being administered, he was not only back to his old self but, better still, the dominant female had clearly got the message that reginal rule in that pen was over. There were no more infertile eggs from their aviary that year.

Chapter Three

'There is a passion for hunting something deeply implanted in the human breast.' – Charles Dickens, *Oliver Twist*.

'Them's rum ol' buggers, artists,' Tony was heard to remark to Jean one day, while they were having their mid-morning brew-up. Beside them on the kitchen table lay a squashed hedgehog, assorted squirrel skins and the mangled remains of a stoat.

There was no doubt in anyone's mind that his generalization was directed at one wildlife painter in particular. The tall and tousled figure of Timothy Greenwood had first been to visit the farm with a friend more than three years previously and I seem to recollect that my parting words on that occasion had been, 'Do come and see us again if you're ever in this area.' Tim duly returned the following week. Once he had established the fact that the contents of my cellar were passable, that our menagerie was irresistible and we ourselves a reasonably tolerable family, it was only natural for him to move in. He was then about twenty-six years old. Being a Bedouin at heart, he did not exactly take up residence, but Daws Hall became an alternative base to his home in Kent for spasmodic bouts of painting in between forays to remoter areas. For these expeditions his Landrover was his camel and into the back of it were thrown the tools of his trade – assorted shotguns, rifles, cameras, snares, gralloching knives and . . . the occasional pencil or paintbrush.

At first we tended to question whether so much shooting and stalking were essential to the pursuit of art, but Tim quietly and disarmingly stifled our misgivings.

41

'You've gotta know your subject in the field, mate,' he would say, or, 'Look at old Liljefors! He spent half his life clobbering game.' While there was no denying the talent of the great Swedish wildlife painter, who was his idol, what Tim failed to explain was that Bruno Liljefors lived at a time when taxation was minimal and that most of his sporting activities were not only encouraged but actually financed by a wealthy patron. For our part, anyway, it seemed rather churlish to level criticisms at someone who was a permanent purveyor of venison, hares, partridges and so on for the larder, to say nothing of the occasional masterpiece for our walls. We were accordingly only too happy to put up with his lesser eccentricities, like mistaking my only two bottles of first-growth claret for cooking wine during one of his culinary sprees, or deliberately pouring a fresh pot of china tea over a sheet of art paper *and* the dining room table in order to achieve some mysterious tinting effect. There were only rare occasions when Didy and I were forced to remonstrate with our resident artist.

One incident, I recall, was when Tim had returned from a long sojourn in the Highlands of Scotland with his Landrover laden to the roof with a mass of trophies in varying stages of decomposition. As soon as the vehicle ground to a halt outside the back door, a great swarm of bluebottles and lesser flies descended on the contents.

'For heaven's sake, don't bring all that garbage into the house,' Didy shouted in horror, as Tim struggled to retrieve a couple of brace of grouse for our supper from underneath his sleeping bag.

Tim grinned his agreement, though I thought I heard him muttering something about ' . . . sort out the old cat while you lot are out of the house tomorrow.'

On our return from a rather smart luncheon party the following afternoon, we were greeted by the most appalling smell.

'Tim! Where are you, Tim?' we shouted in unison, fighting our way into the kitchen through pungent clouds of smoke. And then, having succeeded in opening a window and removing a charred saucepan devoid of all liquid from the stove: 'Where's that bloody artist?'

It was at that precise moment that our young and talented friend strolled nonchalantly in through the back door, shotgun under his arm and the glazed eyes of several lifeless rabbits protruding through the network compartment of his game-bag. When he saw that we were home, his expression quickly changed.

'Cor, you're b-back early,' he stammered, glancing anxiously first at us and then at the stove. 'I was, er, just hoping to get a little boiling-up job done before you returned.'

There followed a short but distinctly uncomfortable silence. During this time Tim shifted uneasily from leg to leg, his face changing colour like the aurora borealis, while Didy's eyes narrowed and her teeth clenched as she tried, at one and the same time, to control her temper and to assess the damage. When she finally uttered I found it hard to relate her normal dulcet tones to the rasping, vituperative sound that emerged.

'What the hell do you mean by ruining my best non-stick saucepan?' she screamed. 'You really are the most irresponsible, hopeless, idiotic, senseless, addle-pated nitwit I've ever met.' At that, to Tim's relief, she appeared to run out of steam.

'Um, er, um . . .' he started pathetically, but, before he could offer anything more coherent, Didy had regained her breath and loosed off the second barrel.

'I know what you've done,' she shouted. 'You boiled up those horrible rabbits for the dog and then you went off shooting and forgot all about them.'

Even at this late stage Tim could, with a bit of luck, have emerged from the battlefield reasonably unscathed. His one hope, I realized, lay in pleading guilty to what was technically a false accusation.

'But, I haven't been boiling up rabbits,' he murmured. It was a grave tactical error.

'Well, what the . . .' Didy began, before subjecting the scorched remains of the saucepan to a closer inspection. The smoke by now was beginning to disappear and the most horrible looking apparition, exuding a sickening smell, was clearly discernible in the midst of the mundungus.

'Sorry, Didy,' Tim blurted out. 'It's just the head of an old wildcat . . .'

Slowly the awful truth emerged. Tim had shot the animal in the north of Scotland several weeks previously. It had been his intention to present the skull to a scientist friend, who collected such objects, but the daily rigours of *la chasse* had somehow left him little time to deal with the fundamental business of removing fur, flesh, eyeballs and so on from this trophy. The carcase had accordingly remained in the Landrover all this while and now his plans for 'a quick boiling-up job' had badly misfired. He was, of course, eventually forgiven . . . after presenting Didy with a little pictorial gem in atonement.

Tim had owned some form of lethal weapon for as long as he could remember. By the time he was twelve years old he had become extremely proficient at archery. Staying with his grandmother at Deal one winter, he had crept from the house early one morning armed with home-made bow and arrows for some quiet poaching on a nearby pond. By the time that most people were beginning to stir, Tim was safely home with a mallard, a moorhen and a water-rat proudly tucked inside his shirt. The old lady, although unenthusiastic about the last two items, was delighted to see the duck.

'Go and put it in a cold place in the bathroom, Timothy,' she had said, 'and I'll cook it for our dinner tomorrow.'

Tim had promptly gone off to the bathroom and, reckoning that the coolest place was on top of the lavatory cistern, had climbed onto the seat and duly deposited the bird. An hour later there was a terrible scream from the bathroom. Poor Grannie had pulled the plug and the dead duck had fallen on her head.

His interest in art had been evident from a very early age.

During his last two years in primary school, he spent most of his time painting the scenery for school plays, and consequently failed his eleven plus. At secondary school he came under the kindly wing of the biology master, who was quick to realize that here was one of nature's children. Young Tim would stay behind, when class was over, to help feed the locusts, grass snakes and hamsters. He made up his mind that when he grew up he would be a biology research worker.

Technical school, to which he went at the age of thirteen, was an unhappy contrast. Discipline and conformity reigned supreme and the teachers did not take kindly to the tall, gangling youth on whose unruly mop of hair perched a pair of orphaned goldfinches. While still at school he sold his first paintings. Four garden birds, designed for Christmas cards, netted him £40 and on the strength of this untold wealth his intended career changed overnight to wildlife artist. Remarkably, he was sacked from both art schools that he attended. His ability, he was told, was insufficient to warrant any further time or tuition being given to him. In spite of these early setbacks, he had sufficient confidence in his own talent to persevere. The expression of his art, he was well aware, could only come from increased field observation.

In the spring of 1968 he read an advertisement for volunteers to guard the nest of a pair of snowy owls on Fetlar, a remote island in the Shetlands. Tim applied for the job and was accepted. For five months he and his young companions, three boys and a girl, lived in a dilapidated bothie. Beds consisted of antediluvian iron frames with a cushioning of old newspapers on which they laid their sleeping bags. The only table, on which he executed some of his best paintings to date, was a broken barn door on makeshift legs. One painting in particular still bears witness to this primitive studio. He was just completing a watercolour and pastel of a male snowy owl feeding on a rabbit when an empty whisky bottle fell into the rubbish bin beside him, showering him and the painting with tea leaves and a variety of other debris. In spite of a drastic mopping up operation, a few scars and blemishes still remain to tell the story.

The five months on Fetlar were the turning point in his life as an artist. It marked the beginning of his fascination for birds of prey (or 'raptors'), and it was there that he learned to work from accurate observation of his subjects in the field, rather than relying on photographs and skins as he had done in his early days. He began to experiment with and became proficient in a wide variety of artistic skills – oil, pastel, watercolour, etching and even sculpture – sometimes mixing his media, but always trying to portray the wild birds and animals in accurate and natural settings. Less than four years after his ignominious discharge from art school, he topped the £2,000 mark for a painting for the first time.

It was entirely through Tim that we got to know Pooky and Fuzzy.

'Is that the bird breeders?' A man had enquired on the telephone one Sunday afternoon just as the three of us were finishing our lunch. It was a question that we had heard with increasing frequency ever since we had rashly agreed to be listed in the Yellow Pages of the local telephone directory.

Somewhat cautiously, I admitted that we did in fact keep a few ornamental waterfowl and pheasants. If previous enquiries were anything to go by, I was prepared to wager a small sum that the next question would be either 'I've found a sparrow with a broken wing,' or 'How can I get my mynah bird to talk?'

I should have lost my bet.

'I'm ever so sorry to trouble you,' the man continued, 'but there's an albatross just landed in my herbaceous border. Would you like it?'

The totally matter of fact way in which he had announced the presence in his garden of the bird with the largest wing-span on earth left me speechless. Even allowing for thermal currents and the legendary tales that have surrounded this creature since long before Coleridge's *Ancient Mariner* I could not see how any self-respecting albatross could possibly have come to rest in a bed of delphiniums and michaelmas daisies

46

in East Anglia.

'An albatross?' I eventually repeated rather limply.

At the mention of the word albatross Tim almost spilt his cup of coffee over the Sunday papers.

'An albatross?' He reiterated. 'Some fool needs to have his bloody eyesight tested.'

Further discussion with our enquirer produced no proper clues by which we could establish the bird's identity. We merely learned that it was like a huge and hungry seagull, apparently with a penchant for biting anyone who came within range.

If only to satisfy ourselves that it was *not* an albatross, Tim and I left Didy to dispense the afternoon feed and, piling into his Landrover, set off on our own special snark hunt. On the way, Tim told me that recent research had shown that the albatross's enormous wingspan does in fact enable it literally to circle the earth, but only in very southerly latitudes. There, gliding on winds of around 50 to 60 knots, it is perfectly possible for the bird to fly round the world in eighty days, with considerably less effort than Jules Verne's hero.

'Anyway, apart from very occasional sightings off Southern Ireland or Dungeness, they don't come within hundreds of miles of this country,' Tim announced with authority. 'I reckon what we're going to find is an old black-back.'

We crossed over the Stour and after a couple of miles turned up a narrow lane until we came to a thatched Tudor cottage on top of a rise. As we turned into the gateway we looked back, along hedgerows of hawthorn, ash and elm, into the valley made famous by so many Constable paintings. On the water meadows the graceful symmetry of the willow trees, swaying in the wind, was accentuated by the late afternoon shadows. Close to the weir, like a large diurnal moth, a barn owl floated on silent, ghostly wings. It was October, and the sedge warblers, sand martins, cuckoos and other summer visitors to the water meadows were by now winging their way southwards to warmer climes. The previous day and night there had been easterly gales and a quick glance at dark clouds scurrying in from the direction of the North Sea told us that more foul weather would soon be upon us.

Our reverie was suddenly interrupted.

'Good afternoon, gentlemen. I presume you have come to remove our ferocious bird?'

He was a small man, dapper and middle-aged, and from his manner and appearance I took him to be a schoolmaster or perhaps a civil servant who commuted daily to Ipswich or Chelmsford.

'I trust,' he continued, 'that our identification is correct. I must admit that I'm not a bird-watcher myself, but Mabel – that's my wife – is very keen and she says that she's sure its an albatross. Her childhood was spent in a fishing village in Sutherland where she says she remembers seeing them diving from the cliffs into the sea.'

Sensing a verbal explosion from Tim, I kicked him hard on the shins, but it had little effect. The gist of his next remark, which was fortunately uttered in a muffled voice, was that the bird was a –ing gannet and Mabel was a –ing goon.

Anyway, gannet or loon, albatross or gooney bird, it meant the same thing to Tim as it did to me – a new challenge in the form of a helpless wild creature that had been blown inland and was now going to rely entirely on us for its livelihood.

We found it sitting forlornly at the edge of one of the flower-beds. It looked hungry and dejected and its breast feathers were caked with dirt. I had never before seen a gannet at such close quarters. It was about the size of a snow goose and not dissimilar in colouring, apart from its head which was pale sulphur yellow. Its most salient feature, however, was its long, cruel beak, which snapped, like a clam, onto my thumb as I bent down to pick it up.

'Ouch!' I yelled, or words to that effect.

With my other hand I tried to prise open its beak. This merely resulted in double agony and a second thumb being

48

gripped between vice-like mandibles.

When Tim came to the rescue and succeeded in forcing the gannet's beak open, the situation was reversed. Now it was his turn to holler, for my two mangled stubby thumbs were replaced by one long and artistic forefinger half way down the creature's gullet. This time I seized a short bit of wood and, using this as a lever, managed to open its beak. Whatever its problems or ailments, they did not appear to affect that part of its anatomy.

It was Tim who came up with the bright idea of how to catch a gannet and keep one's digits intact.

'Here, wave that bit of wood in front of its beak,' he said, 'I'll go round behind it and grab it by the neck.'

Unable to combat this double assault, the bird was soon captured. It was a little thin, its crop was empty, but otherwise it appeared to be healthy.

It had obviously had a battering from the gale which had blown it inland from its fishing grounds along the North Sea. On the way back, we drove through Sudbury and called at the fishmongers. The shop was closed, being a Sunday, but I went round to the back and the owner was luckily at home, feet up watching television. Twenty minutes later we were back at the farm with six fresh herrings and an extremely irate gannet.

Quite how he came to be known as Pooky I cannot remember, but it certainly had something to do with his eating habits. We installed him in one of the small waterfowl enclosures recently vacated by a breeding pair of shelduck. In this there was a small but shallow concrete pond which could be drained and refilled daily with clean water from the bore-hole.

Pooky appeared to view his new home with satisfaction. Having slaked his thirst, he began to peer expectantly at us and the bag of fish with his cruel, pale yellow-green eyes.

I took the first herring out of the bag and held it in front of his beak. Pooky stabbed viciously, knocked the fish into the pond and once again my right thumb was incarcerated.

Clearly, more subtle tactics had to be employed, and once again it was Tim who came to the rescue. After helping to extricate my thumb, he cut a hazel stick, sharpened one end with his ubiquitous hunting knife and shoved it up the herring's hind quarters.

Gannets do not take easily to hand-feeding

With this two foot safety margin, he proffered the fish to our gannet. Pooky stabbed again, more in anger than in

hunger, and at the third attempt Tim guided the herring between his beak. A quick twist retrieved the hazel stick and
the fish disappeared down his throat.

Pooky's appetite was insatiable. After a week his plumage
was restored to its pristine gloss, he was visibly putting on
weight and a large proportion of Didy's housekeeping money
had been spent at the fishmonger's. Fingers and thumbs
were still blue and lacerated and we decided that he had far
outstayed his welcome. Although his wings functioned perfectly, he had no means of launching himself into the air from
his rather cramped enclosure, so we drove him off in a large
hamper to the seaside. When we opened the lid, he hopped
out, threw us a final, unappreciative glance with his jaun-
diced eye and swam off to join his companions in the North
Sea.

It was the following summer, when Angus, Katrina and
Hugh were all with us for the summer holidays, that Fuzzy
took up residence at Daws Hall. A friend rang us up to say
that a large elm tree had been blown down the previous night
and with it a kestrel's nest and two recently hatched fledglings. One was dead. The other, weak and doubtless
famished, was being kept alive on the kitchen stove. Tim,
overhearing snippets from the telephone conversation, was
already jumping up and down with excitement and making
little squeaking noises. The thought of being able to hand-
rear a kestrel was proving almost too much for him. Then,
suddenly sensing the urgency of the situation, he rushed out
of the house and leapt into his Landrover almost before I had
handed him the address and replaced the telephone on the
hook.

'Hey, Tim, wait for me!' came the shrill voice of Hugh as
he raced out in pursuit. Although only six, he had always
been the most adventurous of the three and a confirmed dis-
ciple of Tim's.

The other two children adopted their own forms of approach to the impending arrival of the fledgling. While
Angus, the oldest at nine, disappeared into the library to

carry out a little private research on the habits and feeding requirements of kestrels, Katrina busied herself with the domestic arrangements. The most important thing, she decided, was to make a proper nest for the baby. First, she found a small cardboard box and then she set off in search of suitable lining for it. Soon all was ready and there was a shout of, 'Come and look, Daddy, quick!'

Father came at the double as instructed and found the box filled to overflowing with a mixture of doll's clothes and cotton wool from Didy's dressing table. At that moment the sound of screeching brakes and flying gravel announced the landrover's return. Within seconds Hugh was out and into the kitchen.

'Mummy, Iain, we've got it and it's lovely and it's called Fuzzy and Tim thinks it's a girl and he says I can help to feed it and the next one will be my very own and, and, and . . .'

His flow was cut short by the emergence of Tim himself through the door, knitted hat as always perched on his head, hunting knife dangling from his waist and two long, sinuous arms clutching the precious booty that was enveloped in his sweater. Further happy squeaks and grins from him confirmed the success of the operation.

Under Hugh's supervision, Fuzzy was gently removed from Tim's jersey and introduced to Katrina's nest. Apart from two huge eyes and a funny little curved bill she was just a bundle of pale brown fluff, about the size of a powder-puff. Food was obviously the first requirement. Katrina got hold of the milk jug, Angus proclaimed 'field mice and voles' in an authoritative voice, while Tim and Hugh (between whom there had clearly been some collusion on the way home) simultaneously announced 'liver'. All eyes turned on Didy.

'Bang goes our liver and bacon for supper!' she declared in tones of mock distress.

Angus quickly volunteered to give up his share to Fuzzy, until Hugh very sagely pointed out that 'Fuzzies have only got teeny-weeny tummies.'

With enormous patience and emulating the mewing noise

of the parent birds, Tim dangled and waved the first morsel in front of the tiny kestrel's bill. Fuzzy followed the meat backwards and forwards with her eyes and at last gave a little answering squeak and opened her beak. Before she knew what had happened there was a piece of raw liver in her mouth and, presto, it had disappeared. The next two pieces went down without any problem, then she closed her eyes and went fast asleep in the little box at the end of the kitchen table.

At tea time the children vied with each other for the best Fuzzy-viewing chairs. After a bit of argument they sorted themselves out, Katrina in the middle and the two boys on either side. For a while the only noise from that end of the table came from hearty munching of bread and butter, honey from our own bees and chocolate biscuits. Suddenly, the silence was shattered by a shrill scream from Katrina.

'Ugh!' she shrieked, looking down at a jet of creamy white liquid that had landed on her lap.

'Poopers!' yelled Angus.

'Bigs!' came the cry from their step-brother.

'Well, she's got to park it somewhere, hasn't she, mate?' was Tim's contribution, as he shovelled another cucumber sandwich into his own mouth.

While Didy carried out mopping-up operations on Katrina's jeans, Angus laid a trail of newspaper from the edge of Fuzzy's box to the French windows, thus catering for any such missiles as might emerge from a fully grown golden eagle. Fuzzy, having satisfactorily discharged the remains of her first meal at Daws Hall, turned round in her box and went back to sleep.

Under Tim's care, Fuzzy's appetite and size increased by leaps and bounds. So, too, did the volume and range of the guided missiles. After about ten days the soft down began to be replaced by tiny feathers on her back and shoulders and there were visible signs of sprouting tail feathers. The box on the kitchen table remained her nest and Tim spent a large part of each day talking to her, feeding her and making detailed sketches of her progress. From liver she graduated to pieces of chopped rabbit, and mice which the children trapped in the foodshed on the farm. This meant that there was now a new source of waste-disposal in the form of pellets (or castings), which consisted of regurgitated pieces of undigested food – fur, bones and so on – a habit common to all birds of prey. On the four mornings a week when Jean came in to help with the housework, there was always frantic activity just before her arrival to remove all offending objects from the floor and the kitchen table.

Within six weeks Fuzzy's first moult was complete and her newly grown wing-feathers, though still very weak, led her to believe that the time had come to practise the art of flying. Head and neck stretched out, claws firmly gripping the edge of the table for security, she would flap her wings frantically for several seconds before finally launching herself into the air. The first attempt was disastrous and she crash-landed only a couple of feet from take-off. Thereafter, egged on by the children, who waited at ranges of from one to six feet with arms out-stretched for perches, her confidence and ability gradually improved. Her first major accolade was achieved at eight weeks of age when she succeeded in flying unaided up to the big oak beam that spanned the length of the kitchen.

It was under this beam, which dated from the time the house had been constructed in Tudor times, that the kitchen table was sited. It was not long before Fuzzy abandoned Katrina's box and adopted the beam as her new home. Not only was it a comfortable roosting place, but it afforded an ideal position from which she could watch all the comings and goings in the house. Whenever we gathered together for meals, she would sidle along from her usual perch near the window so as to be positioned immediately over the kitchen table. Our meals soon became chaotic and it was a case of either playing a new version of musical chairs, wearing a wide-brimmed hat or hoping for the best. The children, needless to say, found it all hilarious and would break into

Under Tim's watchful eye, Fuzzy grew healthy and strong and was soon attempting flight

'*Raindrops keep falling on my head ...*' every time a fresh avalanche descended on us. The only person who seemed totally unmoved was Tim, in whose eyes Fuzzy could do no wrong. Eventually, by popular request, he was cajoled into training her to sit on his shoulder and comparative peace was restored.

Fuzzy's increasing appetite made it necessary for Tim, with Hugh at heel, to go off most evenings with shotgun or ·22 rifle to the water meadows at the far end of the farm. There rabbits abounded and often they came back with the odd magpie, jay or other vermin. Foxes were the biggest potential threat to the birds on the wildfowl farm and, with the co-operation of the local Hunt (together with various other measures) we usually succeeded in keeping them down to manageable proportions.

That particular summer a lot of cubs had been born in the thickets alongside the railway line, in the pine wood and on several steep, sandy banks where brambles and bracken provided camouflage for their earths. Trails of feathers from wild pheasants, mallard, herons and all sorts of other birds were a common sight along the water meadows and across the rides in the forestry plantations. Then, one night, a fox raided Cees's collection of chickens and ducks that he kept in an enclosure just behind the cottage. Every one of his beloved Dutch call ducks was killed. War was declared and Tim, Cees and I set a series of snares, tethered by stout wire to the eight foot high perimeter fence that surrounded our own waterfowl and pheasants. Within a week the population had been reduced by three vixens. Any fox that was caught was quickly spotted by Cees on his twice daily feeding rounds, so suffering was reduced to a minimum.

Didy and I had for some time been discussing with Tim a suitable subject in oils for a large canvas he had recently bought, and he suddenly came up with the idea of painting a fox cub against the natural background of the water meadows bordering the Stour. We both agreed that it sounded an excellent idea. What we failed to remember was that Tim always liked to paint from life . . .

Early the following morning, just after the children had gone back to school, Cees was seen striding into the kitchen in his size sixteen gumboots, a huge grin on his face and a dead fox cub in his hand.

'Number four,' he announced in triumph, holding it aloft for all to see.

The expression on Tim's face, as he looked up from his cornflakes, can only be described as that of a man watching someone holding out a cheque for his record winnings on the football pools. Didy, scrambled egg in mouth, was clearly having trouble deciding whether to swallow or disgorge.

'Ooch, Didy, I'm sorry,' Cees said, suddenly seeing her reaction. 'I vill go off and bury him.'

This was too much for Tim who rushed forward, seized the dead fox cub and clutched it to his bosom. A few minutes later Jean arrived and, after one look from her, Tim bolted into the garden, canvas under one arm and cub under the other. For the rest of the day he was happy at work under the old mulberry tree on the lawn.

It was a large canvas and even after two days of hard work much detailed brushwork remained to be done. It was mid-summer, but Tim seemed quite unperturbed by the swarms of flies that surrounded his model, which was propped up in a very realistic position against a croquet hoop. Fortunately for us, the wind was in the right direction.

On the third morning Didy and I drove off straight after breakfast to go into Colchester. I had to give a talk to a local luncheon club, Didy wanted to do some shopping. In the afternoon we were due to meet an aged relation of Didy's off the train from London. As we left the house there was a sudden crack of thunder and a few miles down the road the heavens erupted.

'Poor Tim,' murmured Didy. 'That will put paid to his fox painting for a while.'

Aunt Isabel, who was on her way to stay with a sister in Norfolk, was due to spend just one night at Daws Hall. I had never met her, but Tim and I had been carefully briefed by Didy, not only about her likes and dislikes, but on how we ourselves were to behave. 'I'm afraid she's still living in the Edwardian Age,' Didy had said. 'So elbows off the table at mealtimes, no swearing and,' (turning to Tim) 'no rabbits, hares or moorhens on the kitchen floor, please.'

For several days there had been a flurry of activity. Spiders that for generations had happily spun their silken webs over the drawing room ceiling were ruthlessly dislodged and destroyed by Jean, linen napkins were unearthed from long-forgotten boxes in the attic and threaded into their silver rings, and Tim promised faithfully to put on a clean shirt and tie for dinner. While most of the preparations were going on, I conveniently found all sorts of odd jobs to do at the furthest end of the farm. Only on the eve of her visit did I begrudgingly agree to polish our solitary Georgian decanter and slosh into it some sherry of dubious origin. The final act before we departed had been to supervise Tim moving Fuzzy, together with a day's ration of chopped rabbit, into an aviary on the farm.

Tall, imperious and swathed in dove-grey *crêpe-de-chine*, she alighted from the train with a shrill cry of, 'Porter!' To our amazement, the only visible employee of British Rail leapt to his feet and rushed to her assistance. In no time at all two matching leather suitcases, a pigskin dressing case and tightly-rolled parasol were offloaded from the train and, with her new-found admirer trotting at her heels, she swept down the platform towards us.

'Daarling!' she cried, and Didy was soon enveloped under a wide-brimmed hat, festooned with imitation garden produce. Having disentangled herself from Aunt Isabel's embrace, she made the necessary introductions. Doffing my tweed cap I stepped forward and politely shook hands.

As our retinue emerged through the ticket barrier I saw that the rain had ceased and the sun had come out once more. I had difficulty at first in recognizing our car. It was only when I recalled that Tony had spent half the week removing three years of mud, filth, feathers and other debris that I was able to identify the gleaming red paintwork and polished chrome. While the porter was helping Aunt Isabel into the car, Didy whispered, 'Don't forget that its your job to tip him.'

Frantically, I rummaged in my trouser pockets. There was nothing but a solitary pound note. I quietly muttered some hideous oath and the porter grinned his appreciation. Aunt Isabel's visit had got off to an inauspicious start.

The ten mile drive home, during which Didy and her aunt maintained an incessant dialogue, gave me some warning of what to expect during her visit. Didy, very wisely, chose this opportunity to explain the presence of our resident artist.

'But, my deah, I thought they all lived in Pimlico or on the left bank of the Seine. I do hope you're not allowing your house to be occupied by one of those awful *Bohemians*?' The last word was uttered with the severest possible repugnance.

Didy did her best to reassure her, explaining that Tim was a young wildlife artist of exceptional talent. 'He's rather shy actually,' she added, 'so don't be surprised if he's not terribly forthcoming at first. I hope, too, you won't mind all the shotguns and rifles stacked up inside the back hall'.

'Shotguns and rifles!' exclaimed Aunt Isabel. 'What on earth does he want those for?'

Didy tried patiently to explain, but we were clearly on dangerous ground.

'Your daarling mother led me to believe that your farm was a beautiful sanctuary for all sorts of wild creatures – ducks and geese, pheasants and partridges, otters and foxes . . .'

Mention of the last word and the vision of Tim happily working under the mulberry tree had the dual effect of causing me to almost hit an oncoming lorry and momentarily silencing our visitor. I apologized and looked briefly at Didy. Her pallor, I suspected, was not entirely attributable to my driving.

'Darling,' she said to me after a few minutes, 'I'm sure Aunt Isabel won't mind if you drive in through the *back* gate. That way into the house is nearer to the stairs leading up to her bedroom.' This was not strictly true, but I had got the message.

As we approached the house I slowed down and looked to the right. An avenue of lime trees, parallel to the road, lined the front drive but at that speed one could see parts of the front lawn and the area round the mulberry tree. No sign of Tim or the fox cub and I breathed a sigh of relief. I turned in through the farm gate and drove up to the back door.

As I assisted her out of the car, Aunt Isabel's attention was suddenly caught by one of those giant, sword-leaved yuccas, that throw up their spectacular branches of cream-coloured flowers at irregular intervals in the English climate. Didy and she strolled over to inspect it, while I humped the luggage out of the boot. 'Daarling Leo used to so adore those flowers when we lived in South Americah,' I heard her say, as I struggled into the house.

'Wotcha, mate,' came Tim's familiar cry. 'Back early, aren't yer?'

I was immediately conscious of a foul smell coming from the direction of the kitchen. Dropping the luggage and rushing into the room, I gazed in disbelief at the scene before me. Sitting happily at one end of the table in his knitted hat was our gifted artist; facing him, head propped up with the bread board, was the fox cub.

'Sorry, mate,' he blurted out. 'I've almost finished it, but the bleeding flies drove me indoors.' Then, sensing that I was on the verge of having an apoplectic fit, he said, 'Hey, what's up? It's only two o'clock and auntie isn't due till four. I'll have it all cleared up before . . .'

'Tim!' I interrupted, trying hard to stop my voice breaking into a falsetto shriek. 'Its past four, your blasted watch has obviously stopped and auntie will be in the house any moment. Now for Christ's sake . . .' Breaking off I rushed to the window. Didy and Aunt Isabel had, mercifully, gone

over to the herbaceous border. 'Look, fat-head, I'll rush out
and stall them for as long as I can, but get rid of the flaming
fox, open the windows and squirt aerosol all over the place.'

'What an enchanting garden!' said Aunt Isabel as I
rejoined them, red in the face and sweating from my exer-
tions.

'How very kind of you,' I murmured limply, while deftly
steering her on towards the next flower-bed.

Didy had no difficulty in sensing that some drama had oc-
curred. Luckily, I was able to convey to her the need for de-
laying tactics as Aunt Isabel stooped to proffer aristocratic
nostrils to a rose.

Slowly we walked back towards the house and I motioned
to Didy to take her aunt in through the front door. Nipping
round to the rear of the house, I retrieved the luggage, raced
upstairs with it and then returned to the kitchen. Apart from
an overpowering smell of synthetic lavender, all was well.
There was no sign of Tim and I assumed he was busy bury-
ing the fox somewhere on the farm. We had just sat down to
tea in the drawing room when he came in and joined us. Didy
introduced him and Tim bowed low over the bejewelled

hand that was briefly raised in his direction. He had put on a clean pair of trousers, his finger nails were spotless and his hair, which was plastered down tight onto his scalp, also exuded a rather sickening tang of lavender.

The conversation soon turned to Tim's paintings and Aunt Isabel expressed a desire to see some of his work. Tim went off and fetched a few small etchings and watercolours and she was obviously impressed.

'Tell me, deah boy, what are you working on at present?'

Tim looked briefly at me for guidance. 'I'm, er just finishing a big oil of a fox cub,' he replied.

'A fox cub? How simply enchanting! Do please let me see it.' When Tim had gone off obediently to fetch it, she turned to Didy, 'Do you know, daarling, they are one of my favourite animals? Leo and I, you will remember, lived in the heart of the Quorn country for many years, but we both found hunting such a *brutal* sport.'

The word brutal, I noticed, was uttered with the same intensity of feeling as she had used earlier that afternoon when talking about Bohemians.

Tim returned, proudly clutching the huge canvas, and propped it up on an armchair for us all to see. It was faultless, a real masterpiece. For a while we all gazed at it in admiration, absorbing the delicate brushwork, the composition, the tranquility of the water meadows that he had captured so perfectly. It was Aunt Isabel who eventually broke the silence.

'Exquisite talent,' she said with obvious sincerity. 'I think it is absolutely mahvellous. Now do tell me more about it. You must have spent hours watching the daarling creature gamboling among all those deah little daisies. But, wasn't it frightened of you?'

'Well, um, no, er, not really,' Tim replied, shifting uneasily from one leg to the other.

'But they're such shy animals,' Aunt Isabel persisted. 'You must possess such wonderful patience. Anyway, I suppose you modern artists use cameras as well as sketch

62

books. Do you know, when I was a gal, there were some wildlife painters, mostly Germans of course, who killed innocent creatures just to paint them? There was one frightful man called Lilly – something, I think, who . . .'

'Liljefors? He was a Swede,' said Tim, leaping to the defence of his idol. Only a sudden fit of coughing by me prevented him from adding what I knew was on the tip of his tongue, namely that the late-lamented artist was a bloody good bloke.

Didy fortunately seized her cue. 'You must be awfully tired after your journey, Aunt Isabel. Do let me show you your room. Is dinner at eight all right?' With unprecedented alacrity, Tim leapt up to open the door and we both gave an involuntary little bow as she swept regally from the room.

'Phew!' we sighed in unison, before bolting unceremoniously for the drinks tray.

Under Didy's efficient management the rest of her stay went by remarkably smoothly. After breakfast the following morning I gave her a brief tour of the 'daarling birds' and shortly after that Didy took her to the station. By midday we were happily back to normal, Fuzzy mewing in excitement from Tim's shoulder at being released from her temporary prison.

For a while we just sat round the kitchen table, holding the inevitable post mortem that, in all households, follows the departure of guests and eulogizing over Tim's fox painting. There were still a few details to put in around its eyes and on one ear. Otherwise, it was complete.

'Well,' said Didy, 'no *sole meunière* and *crêpes suzettes* for you lads to-day. What's it to be – moorhen *pâté*, bread and cheese or hamburgers?'

Tim and I both opted for a couple of hamburgers and Didy went over to the deep-freeze to get them out.

Suddenly, a high-pitched scream rent the air and I rushed over to see what had happened. For a moment I stared in total disbelief. There, perched on top of some *vol-au-vent* cases and frozen spinach, was the fox cub.

Chapter Four

'A dull speaker, like a plain woman, is credited with all
the virtues, for we charitably suppose that a surface so
unattractive must be compensated by interior blessings.'
– Sir Alan Herbert.

It was not long before Fuzzy, with her new-found powers of
flight, started to venture out of doors. One day a rather
sleepy vole scuttled across the lawn and she made a ludi-
crously unsuccessful attempt to catch it. For most of the
time, however, she was content just to sit on Tim's shoulder,
watching the house martins gathering for migration and
eyeing the sparrows with a hungry look, or she would flap
across the lawn and perch on one of the lower branches of the
mulberry tree, but she was still reliant on us for her food.
There were odd occasions, though, when her zeal exceeded
her aeronautical ability: then, frantic searches would ensue
and one day it took four hours before Didy eventually found
her caught up in a bramble bush at the far end of the vegetable garden.

The rescue and artificial rearing of orphaned creatures
often fails through a combination of ignorance and excessive
enthusiasm, and in Fuzzy's case, we were only too well
aware of the problems that faced us. It is one thing to be able
to shower affection and dead flies on an abandoned swallow
fledgling, but all of this will be wasted if no thought is given
to the bird's eventual release. Kestrels, swallows and other
birds are taught by their parents to fend for themselves in the
wild and their training by humans is often not easy.

With Fuzzy, there appeared to be two alternatives. Either
we committed her to a lonely life and monotonous diet of
dead, day-old chicks in an aviary, or we would have to teach

her to catch live food before returning her to the wild.

Tim was shortly due to go off deer stalking in Scotland, so a decision had to be made fairly rapidly. We carried her out to an empty aviary on the farm and there set about preparing for her eventual release.

House sparrows are a plague on most farms and ours was no exception. Every summer and autumn we trap large numbers and some of these we released in her pen. At first, she was dreadfully hamfisted. Most of the birds succeeded in scuttling out again through the wire, and she would then sit pathetically on her perch, screaming for Tim and her chopped rabbit. The imprinting habit (of which we already had had plenty of experience with Blondie, the female Paradise shelduck, and others) was clearly going to be very hard to break. On Tim's departure for Scotland, however, the situation improved. Cees and I shared the responsibility for her welfare and we intentionally spent as little time with her as possible. Once a day food was brought to her and, apart from the occasional dead mouse, she either had to catch it and kill it, or she went without. Her mewing calls became much less frequent and she was increasingly showing every sign of being capable of fending for herself.

By mid October, when the lime trees along the drive were already bare and the beech and oak leaves had assumed their rich autumn colouring, Tim returned from Scotland with assorted provender for the deep-freeze and some marvellous sketches of golden eagles and ptarmigan. The following morning, we, her human foster-parents, gathered in a sad little group on the lawn to bid Fuzzy farewell. Heading due East, she climbed higher and higher into the sky. At last, when she was just a speck in the distance, we saw her dip down over the poplar trees towards the rich hunting grounds that bordered the river.

It was not only Fuzzy who departed from Daws Hall that autumn. Tim flew to Canada, to hunt and sketch in British Columbia, while Didy and I went to the States. It was my first visit and I had been invited to lecture on the subject of

65

'Birds, Bees and Bedlam'.

The bedlam, it soon transpired, was not confined to Daws Hall Wildfowl Farm. My first talk, to a group of ladies in Virginia, was to be accompanied by colour slides illustrating some of the members of our menagerie. The husband of one of the organizers had kindly volunteered to operate a borrowed projector. After a marvellously hospitable welcome and a short introduction, the lights were turned out and I gave the signal for the first slide to be shown. There was an appreciative hum from the audience as a shot of the front of our house, with nesting black swans in the foreground, appeared on the screen. The picture was sharp, the focusing perfect. After a brief description of the typical Georgian architecture, I was about to comment on the birds. With no cue from me, however, the slide suddenly changed and we were all looking at Cobus, our original male Vietnamese pot-bellied pig. It was a disappointing start, especially as I had wanted to tell a story about the swans; one that could invariably be guaranteed to raise a laugh. Never mind, I said to myself, there was a slide of black cygnets towards the end and I could relate the story then. Anyway, there had been plenty of amusing incidents with our pigs.

Several years previously Cees had persuaded us to try and buy a pair of these ridiculous creatures from the East, with their wrinkled faces, stunted legs and bellies that drooped to the ground. For a long time it appeared that there was just one specimen in the whole of the British Isles, an ancient boar that resided in solitary splendour at Whipsnade Zoo. Cees had been to visit him and it was he who had christened the beast Cobus, explaining to Didy and myself that it was Dutch for dirty old man. Until such time as a sow or gilt could be located, we had no means of knowing whether he would ever live up to his name. Finally after months of searching, we had found a wife for him in the north of England, but for Cobus the strain and excitement was too much. He had promptly expired while astride her.

It was a risqué story, better suited perhaps to an after-dinner speech to Round Tablers in England than to an untried, all female audience that comprised many of the local aristocracy of Norfolk, Va. If the tale of our homosexual black swans had gone down well, I might have tried it, but, given the circumstances, decided to confine myself to reminiscences of our chasing escaped piglets through the flower-beds. I was just reaching the punch line, when Cobus's ugly face vanished without warning from the screen and a group of baby ducklings appeared in its place. There was a polite ripple of laughter from the audience, but I sensed that it was not entirely attributable to my tale of the pot-bellied piglets.

To my relief, the changing of the next three slides was executed with perfect precision. My delivery became more confident and the Virginian ladies and their speaker, were, I felt, gradually beginning to warm to one another.

Slides six to eight showed three stages of my climbing a tree after a swarm of bees and returning them to the hive. The first of these was upside down and I was displayed balanced on my head in mid air, with a branch glued to the soles of my feet and a cluster of bees nine inches from my nose. That brought the first proper laugh of the afternoon.

'Could you,' I enquired of the projectionist, 'possibly turn that one round, please?'

This apparently, was easier said than done. A button was pressed and the audience had a brief preview of the next six slides flashing in quick succession before their eyes. Then, with equal rapidity, the machine went into reverse and we were back with Cobus and the black swans. At last the offending slide was located, re-positioned, and this time I was horizontal, stretched out at right angles towards the bees, like a trapeze artist in a space suit or a rather portly stick insect.

The projectionist apologised, but it was my fault, as I should have checked the machine and the loading of the slides beforehand. The slightest touch on the trigger mechanism sent snow geese and shovellers, peacocks and piglets galloping chaotically across the screen, as I struggled in vain to throw in a brief word or two of identification.

Speaking in public is something that comes easily to very few. The best (and often seemingly impromptu) talks are almost invariably carefully rehearsed. When well delivered, they can be equally rewarding to speaker and listener, while (as all of us have discovered to our cost) a second-rate speech or slide show is as painful and embarrassing an experience as one can suffer. One original piece of advice that I received many years ago was 'talk as long and as often as you possibly can, for in this way you will soon acquire that natural contempt for your audience that every bore instinctively has.'

For my own part, I had for a number of years given illustrated talks to local Women's Institute and natural history groups for fees that barely covered the cost of my petrol. Then, one day, a friend said why didn't I make a respectable charge and get taken on by an agent.

'Me? An agent? I thought they only handled film stars or television personalities.'

'Not at all,' he had replied and promptly gave me a name and telephone number to contact.

It turned out to be one of the leading lecture agencies in the country and, much to my surprise, I was immediately enrolled as one of their speakers. Their brochure was an impressive document. The directors were well known in show-biz circles and all but one of their speakers seemed to be household names. That exception was me.

Presiding, like a mother hen over this assorted brood, was a large and lovable ex-nurse from County Cork. She explained to me, in her rich Irish brogue, that she was the link woman between all their speakers and numerous clubs and organizations up and down the country. Bookings, fees, overnight accommodation, last minute cancellations – all of these were in her capable hands. So, too, was an annual luncheon at the Dorchester Hotel in London, where representatives of ladies' luncheon clubs and the like had the chance to meet and assess prospective speakers.

It was with some trepidation that Didy and I stepped through the imposing portals of the hotel for the first time. We were each given badges proclaiming our names and then directed to one of the large reception rooms where a group of over a hundred men and women, wearing similar lapel badges, were drinking and talking. A quick look round the assembled gathering was sufficient for us to realize that in most cases identification badges were superfluous. Politicians, racing motorists, actors and sports commentators jostled and joked with one another, as we sidled surreptitiously into a corner with our glasses of tomato juice.

Suddenly, the volume of voices rose to a climax. The doors opened and we were engulfed by what John Knox aptly termed 'the monstrous regiment of women'. Bonneted and and bejewelled, they advanced upon us, each carrying a catalogue of the speakers.

'What do you talk on?' 'Do you require overnight hospitality?' 'Are you funny?' These and other questions were showered upon us and we hardly had time to reply before some inglorious mark had been made against our names in the catalogue and a new inquisitor was accosting us. For the first time in my life I began to appreciate what bullocks might feel like at a cattle market.

After half an hour of acute misery, spent mainly in watching the famous consulting their engagement diaries, we were ushered into the banqueting hall. There a series of separate tables accommodated one or two speakers to approximately ten of our prospective clients. Glancing over my shoulder, I noticed that our fellow speakers were all liberally dispensing wine to their admirers. I fumbled in my trouser pockets and found some loose silver, the car keys and a couple of return tickets to Colchester. Didy, seeing my predicament, smiled sympathetically, well knowing that I had had to borrow her last fiver for the train fares. Our table drank water and that year I did not receive a single enquiry.

Paddy, the Irish lady, had in fact warned me that it

might take a little while before I received the first booking and explained that most clubs organized their programmes a year in advance. 'Iain, me darlin, we're plugging you loike mad and it's just a question of toime,' she said, in that soothing voice that must have calmed many a hospital patient.

Next summer, when it was time once more to attend the annual get-together in London, we again bought two tickets in advance. At the end of these lunches several new speakers were always invited to get up and talk for two minutes. 'If only I could be *heard* . . .' I kept saying to myself, while driving to the bank the previous day to cash an enormous cheque. Fate, however, decreed otherwise and we had to cancel the lunch and visit a sick relation instead.

'Paddy,' I said to her on the telephone, when yet another year had gone by and there were still no engagements, 'you're wasting printers' ink including me in your brochure; I really think you ought to scrub my name off the list.'

She would not hear of it, however, insisting that I was one of her most precious untried assets. Her optimism and blarney amazed me.

Once again the day came for the annual gathering at the Dorchester. Sitting in the train, I scanned the newspapers, while mulling half-heartedly over what I might say in the unlikely eventuality of my name being drawn out of the hat. No inspiration came to me, only the realization that expensive lunches in London's West End and the forcing of alcohol down unknown, thirsty throats from Doncaster, Torquay and Newcastle-upon-Tyne were luxuries that I could ill afford.

As I strode up to the table to collect my lapel badge, Paddy's unmistakable voice floated across the foyer towards me. 'Iain, now there you are! Your name's been drawn and you're first to speak.' A wave of panic enveloped me. Sick with terror, I bolted for the Gents.

Perched on the seat in this tiny cubicle, with no distraction save for occasional water music, I struggled to compose something presentable. My mind, however, remained blank.

Had I not been a coward by nature and a Scot by birth, I would have fled forthwith into the street, sacrificing both my ticket and my reputation for a quiet sandwich in a pub. Then, suddenly, a spark of inspiration! Why not tell the story of Blondie, the duck who fell head over heels in love with me? I hastily scribbled some notes on a sheet of the nearest available paper, then tried it once on myself – the story that is, not the paper – and a distant cistern gurgled its approval.

When I rose to speak at the end of the lunch, my legs were quivering like jelly and I felt convinced that my voice-box was paralyzed. In some astonishing way, however, intelligible words came forth and my talk was greeted with much applause. I had, it seemed, won my spurs, for thereafter Paddy was on the telephone incessantly with invitations to speak in every corner of the British Isles. A confirmed countryman, I suddenly found myself travelling at someone else's expense to towns that I had never previously visited. Manchester and Birmingham became more than places on the map, while the ladies from the Dorchester were no longer bogies, but kind and warm-hearted human beings.

Apart from acute attacks of stage-fright that I felt (and still feel) every time I address an audience, I was fortunate in having only one really uncomfortable experience. A ham-fisted waitress in a hotel in Leicester deposited the contents of a gravy bowl in my lap shortly before I rose to speak. Having the entire attention of some hundred ladies focused, not on my face, but my sodden midriff for forty-odd minutes was disconcerting to say the least.

After a busy but enjoyable six months on the lecturing circuit in Britain an invitation came to visit the States. From Virginia we flew north to New York, the area purchased from the Indians by Dutch traders in 1626 for twenty-four dollars worth of trinkets. The sheer vastness of the United States of America is something that strikes all newcomers, particularly those from our own small island. It is not just the magnitude and diversity of its three million square miles, nor

71

even its towering skyscrapers, its six-lane freeways or majestic scenery; perhaps more than all of these, it is the Americans' own concern with size. To the early settlers, this enormous uncharted land mass, stretching three thousand miles from ocean to ocean, matched the challenge, the dangers and the opportunities open to them. The vastness, which was then the creed for survival, is now the testimony to American ambition and success. This philosophy, which still serves as an inspiration to both college boy and tycoon, no doubt prompted Oscar Wilde's infamous remark: 'The youth of America,' he wrote, 'is their oldest tradition. It has been going on now for three hundred years.'

Low-slung and ultra-modern, our hotel on Long Island contained everything but the simple essentials. The windows in our over-heated bedroom were clearly not designed for fresh air-loving eccentrics, while on the dining room tables, the notices on plastic 'milk' cartons reassured us that the contents were an 'ultra-pasteurized, non-Dairy product.' Apart from this, everything was splendid. The beef steaks were huge and well-hung, the fish superb and, at the bar, we were painlessly anaesthetized by successions of intoxicating 'stingers'. We also had time for a quick dip in the luxurious swimming pool.

On the morning after our arrival we went for the usual sight-seeing tour. It was an impressive and enjoyable experience, until the moment came for me to pay off the cab driver. My passport and note case containing money and travellers' cheques were not in my breast pocket. I realized I must have forgotten to take them out of the suit I had been wearing the previous day. Didy, fortunately, had some ten dollar bills in her bag, but in the circumstances we thought it wise to curtail our tour and return to the hotel forthwith.

There an unpleasant shock was in store for us. My other pockets were empty too. After half an hour's fruitless search, which revealed nothing but sinister scratch marks round the lock on the door, we decided to report the loss. I sent a telegram to my bank in England, instructing them to cancel the cheques, and then I rang the local police station. We had not long to wait. The measured tread of heavy boots was heard approaching down the corridor and there was a loud knock on our door.

Had we not been addicts of the famous television series, we should not have believed the sight that met our eyes. Standing foursquare in the doorway, hands poised for the proverbial quick draw, was Kojak's big brother.

'Oh, how do you do? I'm Mrs Grahame. Won't you come in?' He was not only in by then, but lowering his huge frame onto the edge of the bed. One hand reached for notebook, form and pencil, while the other adjusted his armoury. With two revolvers, truncheon and other pieces of equipment, he was armed for a latterday Custer's last stand.

'What's yer name?' He fired. I told him.

'Say dat again.' I did, but the pencil never moved and the big brows furrowed. 'What's yer foist name?'

'Iain,' and I spelt it for him.

A pause, then, 'I t'ought you said something before that.'

'Yes, Major; that's my rank. Well, actually I'm retired now, but I still use it. If you want my profession, I breed ornamental birds.'

'Hey, you some kinda nut?'

'I beg your pardon?'

'Ah mean are you serious or are you putting me on?'

Didy leaped to my rescue. 'Oh, no, officer,' she explained, 'that really is what we do. In fact on Friday we're attending a special bird breeders convention here on Long Island.'

He scratched his head for a moment, looking at us with obvious disbelief, then asked where we came from. I gave him our address.

'Suffolk?' he said, and for the first time the trace of a smile came over his face. 'That sounds like where some of ma folks come from. Sure is nice to meet you, sir.' He rose to his feet. 'You too, ma'am,' fumbling with his peak cap.

We, too, smiled our appreciation and I murmured something about it being a small world. And yet, somehow, I could not quite see our new-found friend's relations fitting into the quiet backwaters of East Anglia. Then, suddenly it came to me. 'Oh, you mean from one of the American Air Force bases?' and I enumerated them, one by one – 'Bentwaters, Lakenheath, Mildenhall . . . ?'

The law once again look puzzled and I realized there must be some misunderstanding. 'What part of Suffolk?' I asked him.

'What do you mean: what part of Suffolk? Suffolk, Long Island, New York.'

'Oh, but we come from a different Suffolk,' I laughed. 'The one on the other side of the Atlantic.'

There was an embarrassed pause, then he sat down once more, slowly this time, and the ironware jangled against the bedstead. 'I did realize that. Now, yer full *add*ress.'

I gave it to him – house, village, county and country.

'England?' It was the last word that seemed to be puzzling him most.

'You know, Britain, er, Great Britain,' I added, feeling a sudden surge of patriotism.

'You mean England, *Europe*?'

'England, Europe', I confirmed and then went on to give him a brief account of my stupidity in leaving all my valuable possessions in the hotel room. At the end I showed him the scratch marks against the lock and suggested that there seemed to have been a burglary while we were out. 'Perhaps there are finger prints there that will give you a clue?' I said.

Kojak major, however, was not impressed by amateur detective work and went on writing. Glancing over his shoulder, I was relieved to see that the name and address were faultless. There was just one final section of the form to complete. 'Can I see yer passport?' He demanded.

'I told you, its been stolen.'

'Stolen?'

'Yes, stolen'.

'Don't give me no problems. I got to fill in all passport details.'

'Well, I'm very sorry, but I really can't give you any more help.'

Help or reinforcements were clearly needed. He reached for the telephone and dialled a number. 'Hi, it's de big boy; who's squealing?' He drawled. 'Can you put me through to Al?' Then, after a brief pause: 'Say, Chief, ah've got some folk here from England; you know, England, Europe . . .' and began to explain his problem over the passport. He was soon cut short, however, and sharp instructions were barked over the line.

Kojak major looked worried. 'Yessir,' he said, replacing the receiver. He turned to us. 'Sorry, you folks, ah gotta go. Some gal's been raped in the next block. We'll do our best for you.' And with that he hitched up his holsters and clattered from the room.

I went to the bathroom and turned on the taps. Five minutes later, clad in my dressing gown, I walked through from the bedroom. As I thrust my hands into the pockets I felt my missing note-case and passport.

'I think,' Didy murmured, 'that is something that should *not* be reported to the police.'

My talk to the pheasant and waterfowl breeders' convention was scheduled for two days later. We had much to do in the intervening time. There were visits to pay to some well known bird collections in the area, including the Bronx Zoo, and I was also anxious to see a couple of publishers in New York. Tim was due to arrive from Canada the following day and, since I knew he wanted to sell some of his work in the States, I planned to take him with us.

He arrived a day early, and regaled us over dinner with his experiences of flighting duck and hunting moose in the snowy wastes of British Columbia. Before pulling the trigger of his ·375, he had photographed with his two-foot long telephoto lens a huge bull moose, standing broadside-on at a range of over three hundred yards. This photograph, together with the mammoth antlers and skin, eventually found their way to Daws Hall and resulted in one of his finest oil

A magnificent bull moose in British Columbia

paintings.

He was, however, not quite so lucky with a skunk that he found run over on the road, close to the weekend retreat of some very smart friends of Didy's in Manitoba. They had kindly lent him their caravan, which was kept in the northern part of the state, and it was into this that the corpse was at first transferred. Although Tim is normally immune to the more powerful smells of nature, that emanating from the musk glands of the dead skunk was too much even for him. After a couple of days, he skinned the creature, rubbed salt and alum into the hide and placed it on top of the caravan.

The following weekend, his hosts drove out of the city to join him for a couple of days' wildfowling in the fresh open air. Their horror at discovering their beautiful private camping site ruined by skunk smell can well be imagined. Tim was left in little doubt that his visit should be curtailed forthwith. He and the skunk skin were driven in the back of an open truck to Winnipeg, where his hosts generously permitted him to bath and change before depositing him, with considerable relief, at the airport.

Seemingly oblivious of the distress created by his travelling companion, Tim next descended on some friends in Toronto. The skin remained in his suitcase that evening, so at that stage his new hosts had little idea of what was in store for them. The following morning they went off to work, leaving Tim to his own devices. A swift inspection of the house and a washing machine and tumble dryer were located. With complete faith in modern machinery, Tim unwrapped his trophy and placed it in the brand new washing machine. An hour or so later, the washing cycle completed, a seemingly fragrant skin was removed, chucked into the tumble dryer and the second machine switched on. Pleased with the progress, Tim went into the kitchen to make himself a cup of coffee. When he came back and looked through the window, he saw to his horror that the skunk skin was by no means the sole occupant of the dryer. A jumbled heap of pants and

A skunk skin was not an ideal companion for the family wash

pyjamas, shirts and socks, knickers and nightdresses were
whirling round with it.

Worse was to follow. It began to dawn on him that the fragrance of soap was fast disappearing from the room and the
all-too-familiar stench was once again in the air. The washing machine gave the first clue: a close inspection revealed
that skunk hairs had found their way into every nook and
cranny of the machine's interior. When wet, the smell had
been masked, but now the all-pervading odour had returned.

When he opened the tumble dryer an even more terrible
sight met his eyes. Every single item of the household
laundry was covered in black and white hairs. In desperation
he hurled the offending skin into a plastic bag, quickly located some brown paper and string and rushed to the local

Post Office. A small parcel, marked 'Handle with Care' and 'Natural History Specimen for Scientific Study' was consigned by airmail to his mother's home in Kent.

His host had returned home for lunch just before him. 'Funny smell,' he remarked, as Tim stood guiltily in the doorway. 'Anyone would think there was a dead rat or skunk under the floorboards.'

Tim, honest and honourable as always, grovelled his apologies, deposited a masterpiece and fled south to join us in the States.

The following morning Didy, Tim and I set off for the city, taking with us a selection of Tim's paintings and etchings and the synopsis of a new book on which we were working. First on our list of calls was the New York Zoological Society at the Bronx Zoo. After a short train journey as far as the outskirts, we changed over to the subway. Jostled by people of every colour and creed and surrounded by extraneous *graffiti*, we descended further and further into the bowels of the earth until we finally reached the platform to which we had been directed. The train glided to a halt and we jumped aboard. Fortunately, we had the compartment almost to ourselves – just one Black with a deep scar on his cheek and a white couple. For a while the journey passed without incident, then I noticed the couple eyeing us with interest. They got up as we approached the next stop and, as they moved towards the door, the man leaned over towards me. 'Pardon me, sir, but ah guess you must be strangers,' he whispered in a deep Southern drawl. 'Hope you know it can be real dangerous travelling alone with a nigger in this area. Only last week there was a murder right here on the subway. If I were you, mister, I would get out, fast.'

Like scalded cats we leaped to our feet, tore out onto the platform and jumped into the adjoining compartment, just before the doors closed. Sitting at one end was the sole occupant, a huge man who looked like a cross between Sonny Liston and the Boston Strangler.

As we took our seats at the furthest corner from him, Tim

turned to me, 'I've left my etchings in the other carriage.' He had gone rather a nasty shade of grey.

At that moment the man put a hand into one pocket and brought out a knife. My jaw sagged and I felt my knees wobbling. For a moment he seemed to leer in our direction, then he plunged his hand into the other pocket and produced an apple, and neatly carved out the core.

Only Didy looked unperturbed. 'For heaven's sake, pull yourselves together, you two,' she whispered angrily. 'The poor man's only having his lunch. I've never seen two such pathetic and helpless men in all my life. Now, as soon as we get to the next stop, get ready to jump out of this compartment, then you, Tim, nip in and get your wretched etchings, if they haven't already been stolen, and we'll all move into the next compartment up.'

Tim and I needed no second bidding. As soon as the train stopped, we stampeded for the door, all gentlemanly behaviour forgotten, leaving Didy to bring up the rear.

'I'll help you Tim,' I said, feeling a lot less brave than I sounded, and ran with him into our original compartment.

The Black was still there, on his own, and so too were Tim's etchings. Just as Tim grabbed them, the doors closed. I looked around for Didy and thought we had lost her. At last I saw her, through the glass windows, in the compartment in front of us, where she had told us to go. She had the entire place to herself. We sat down on the edges of our seats, feeling like the two babes in the wood.

Scar-face turned to Tim and grinned. 'Hey, man, what's you back foh?'

'I, er, left my p-p-paintings behind.'

'Cool man, what you paint, some noodes?' and he gave a sinister guffaw.

'I think we shall have some rain today, Tim, don't you?' I remarked in a pathetic attempt to change the subject.

Our companion, however, was not to be distracted. 'Lemme see some of them there paintings,' he said, getting up from his seat and standing over us. 'You know, man, ah

80

sure do dig de arts.'

I felt Tim edging closer to me. Reaching into the folder, he handed over a fine etching of a bald eagle. 'N-national bird of the States,' he stammered. Scar-face held it up to the light and nodded his appreciation. Looking up, I suddenly realized that we were at a station and grabbed Tim's arm. Abandoning the etching, we rushed to the exit but again were just too late.

'Hey, what's yer problem?'

'I'm sorry, but we're just trying to join up with my wife,' I explained. 'You see, we've got separated and she's in the next compartment.'

The train rumbled on, gathering speed, and the lights began to flicker. The Black swayed back towards us, paused and then began to shake with terrifying gusts of laughter. It was most unnerving. Tim and I backed away from him, and I prayed that we were close to a station. At last he managed to control himself. 'You sure are a coupla goddam jerks', he drawled. 'All you'se gotta do is walk through dis here door,' and with that he pointed to the communicating door and doubled up with laughter once more. We joined Didy and the journey continued without further loss of dignity.

We walked from the subway station to the zoo, passing through one of the least salubrious areas of New York. Here, the squalid streets and gaunt, grey architecture seemed a fitting backdrop to the expressionless faces of the inhabitants. The Bronx Zoo, by contrast, was a welcome and refreshing oasis and the recently constructed building, housing the 'World of Birds', was a superb example of modern aviary design. Once inside, no glass or wire obstructed one's vision and only the change from light to darkness between interior and exterior precluded the birds from mingling with the public. Tropical sunbirds and humming birds feasted on nectar-giving flowers, while desert species were shown in their own arid surroundings. Only at Antwerp Zoo had we seen such a superb and aesthetically pleasing exhibition, and

81

it was the original Antwerp design that had been copied profitably by the New York Zoological Society and a number of other zoos.

Tim and I vetoed further forays onto the subway, so at the exit from the zoo we hailed a cab and asked the driver to take us to Manhattan. The absence of door handles on the interior of the cab, the bullet-proof glass between us and the driver, and the safety hatch, through which fares and change were passed, gave us a strangely uncomfortable feeling. They served in a way to emphasize the marked contrasts in the different sectors of the city through which we passed, from the silent, yet savage apathy of the Bronx and Harlem to the soaring skyscrapers and bustle of Manhattan.

Our next port of call was a firm of publishers in the Avenue of the Americas, where we had an appointment for two o'clock. Leaving Didy to window gaze and to get some small presents for the children, Tim and I went into the building on our own and took the elevator to the fifty-seventh floor. For a long time he had been trying to persuade me to collaborate over a book on his beloved raptors, or birds of prey. Since the vast majority of the work was to consist of reproductions of his paintings, and since the text was to be reduced to the barest minimum, I had finally agreed to give it serious consideration. The first thing we had to do, however, was to find a publisher who was equally enthusiastic.

I knocked on the door and we were invited to enter. The secretary, who welcomed us, checked our names against the engagement diary and showed us to a couple of seats. 'I'll just see whether Mr Riley is ready to see you,' she said. When she came out of the adjoining room, I thought I detected a rather worried expression on her face. 'I'm terribly sorry, gentlemen, but he's rather, er, tied up. I wonder if you would mind coming back in half an hour?'

Assuring her that this would be perfectly all right, we left our material on a table in her office and returned to street level. Promptly at two thirty we were back.

There was no doubt on this occasion. There was a problem.

'I'm awfully sorry to inconvenience you in this way,' she explained, shifting uneasily from one leg to the other, 'Mr Riley is still, not quite ready to see you. Perhaps I could get you both some coffee?'

Ten minutes later she walked across to his door again and knocked, a little timorously it seemed. There was no reply, so she then opened the door a crack and looked in. A muffled groan emerged. 'Major Grahame and Mr Greenwood to see you, sir,' she announced. Another groan from within and she beckoned us to enter.

Slumped in a chair with his feet on the desk was a portly, red-faced gentleman in his middle fifties. For a moment or two he regarded us with a rather vacuous expression, then motioned us to two chairs that faced him. Tim and I sat down. 'Cigar?' he enquired, clumsily pushing a box of Havanas across the desk, narrowly missing his cup of coffee.

He seemed reluctant to open the conversation, and I reminded him briefly of the project (on which we had already corresponded) and explained that we had brought with us a short synopsis of the proposed book, together with some colour transparencies of Tim's paintings. 'Perhaps you would like to have a look at them?' I said, but he seemed to be having some difficulty in comprehending my remarks and there was a glazed look in his eyes. He was very drunk.

Tim shuffled through his folder and produced a photograph of gyr falcons that he had painted in Norway. 'Adult female on the right and an immature male on the left,' he said, passing it across the desk.

Mr Riley held it up towards the window. It was upside down. Tim and I exchanged glances, a little uncertain of what we should do.

'I'm so sorry, sir,' I said, 'I think we gave it to you the wrong way up.'

He regarded me blankly for a moment then slowly reversed the photograph. Again he peered at it in a vacant fashion, but the strong sunlight was obviously having a disagreeable effect on his eyeballs. Lowering his arm, he

83

knocked over the coffee cup, right into the open box of cigars.

'Where's that G.D. secretary of mine?' he blurted.

Seizing our cue, we picked up our material and made a dignified exit.

Apart from this awkward experience our visit was enjoyable in every way, and the days passed all too quickly. So often there is a spontaneous bond of friendship between people of all races who share common interests and pursuits, and nowhere, it appeared, was this better exemplified than in the States. Kindness, hospitality and liver-ravaging stingers greeted us wherever we went. The convention was well attended, the projector functioned perfectly, and we were able to visit a number of excellent bird collections. While I found it sad to see, except in a very few places, flocks of broody hens and bantams, or any of the old-fashioned game-keeping methods of rearing, we were impressed by the efficiency of their fully automated methods of hatching and rearing. Like their British counterparts, the American aviculturists are extremely conscious of the important role that can be played by small, backyard breeders. Various organizations, such as the American Pheasant and Waterfowl Society, were currently battling with the bureaucrats to obtain official recognition of these captive, self-sustaining collections of endangered species. The 1973 Convention on Trade in Endangered Species (generally known as the Washington Convention), which was designed to control the international movements of these birds and animals has sadly led to much inhibiting legislation, particularly in North America. We found a situation existing whereby breeders, having been unable to extract the necessary licenses to move endangered birds across state boundaries, were forced, through lack of space, to eat their precious eggs.

Very noticeable, in the States was the difference in approach to the 'hunting' of gamebirds and the absence of what, to the British, are traditional sporting attitudes. One charming American thought I was pulling his leg when I explained that we normally allow pheasants to take to their wings before shooting them. We found a markedly wider ideological rift between 'sportsmen' and conservationists in the States than is yet apparent in Britain.

Chapter Five

'Little birds are dining
Warily and well,
Hid in a mossy cell;
Hid, I say, by waiters
Gorgeous in their gaiters –
I've a tale to tell.'
Lewis Carroll, *Sylvie and Bruno*

The year following our return was one of the busiest and most successful seasons on the farm. House martins twittered and toiled outside our bedroom window, two pairs of barn owls floated lazily over the bat willow trees in the water meadows and every morning Cees came into the kitchen to announce the latest births of waterfowl and pheasants. Early in April one of our bantams hatched a solitary Malay peacock pheasant chick. It was a slender contribution to the captive population of this species, but since we held the only pair in the whole of Europe at that time and since the female only lays one egg in a clutch, it was a red letter day. (The male, it may be remembered, was the bird that Cees and Tony had retrieved so spectacularly from a treetop the previous year.)

The poultry we keep are a strange and assorted lot, mostly mongrels, but all containing the blood of silkies or other old-fashioned broody strains in their pedigree. Egg production is of negligible importance and their sole *raison d'être* is to hatch and rear the other creatures on the farm. One year a brood of ducklings may emerge from the eggs on which a broody has been sitting, while another year it could be goslings, pheasants, peafowl or even swans. The incubation periods also vary, some breeds taking as little as eighteen or nineteen days, while for others it can be as long as six weeks. Whatever pops out of the eggs these broodies are expected to feed, protect and keep warm. Many of the older inhabitants of the hen-house are known to us by name. The two senior roosters, Mole and Hop-along Cassidy have been with us since the farm began in 1963. Their enormous spurs alone provide a clue to their great age, but their health and virility remain unimpaired. Mole, small, black and furry, has for his harem the smaller ladies – Peg-leg, Queen Victoria, the *Poellekie*[1] and all their multi-coloured descendants. Hop-along, lame in one leg from an old battle with the neighbour's cat, rules supreme over the matrons of more ample proportions. Senior of these is Bessie Braddock whose obesity has been caused by a mixture of old age, lack of exercise and the raising of hundreds of children. Once a day she ambles off her straw nest for a couple of handfuls of corn, but for the rest of the time she squats in a corner of the hen-house, quietly awaiting the summons to take on a new clutch of eggs. Then there are Dora, Dulcie and Deborah, triplets from her first family, the vociferous skewbald, Hattie Jaques, Baldie, Brunhilde and others.

On Cees's insistence, the Malay peacock pheasant egg had been entrusted to the *Poellekie*. It was many years ago that she had won her spurs by successfully rearing some blood pheasants, the rarest birds in our collection, and since then she had always been held in reserve for particularly valuable eggs. She was the tiniest bantam that we had, and every summer, when we found that she had gone broody, Cees's whole face would become suffused with a seraphic expression.

'Hello, my little *Poellekie*,' he would say, thrusting an enormous forefinger under her tiny body and lifting her from the straw. 'You haf gone broody, haf you? Now ve must find you some lovely leetle eggs to sit on.'

Perched on Cees's finger his treasure would be transported to the adjoining brooder-shed where a clean, fresh nest-box had been prepared for her. Thereafter, every afternoon, when the broodies were taken off their eggs by Cees for their daily exercise and sustenance, his countenance would

---

[1] Dutch for 'my little chick' and pronounced 'poolicky'.

take on this same sublime and rapturous look as he gently opened the door to his favourite box. The *Poellekie*, revelling in this admiration, would hop onto his forefinger and look lovingly into his eyes.

'Ooch, my *Poellekie*, my leetle *Poooellekie*', would be the invariable greeting before he inquired tenderly how life was progressing with her and her solitary, pure white egg.

On the eighteenth day Cees had noticed a tiny chip in the egg and the *Poellekie* had been reluctant to come off the nest. She sat tightly while he gently massaged the top of her head, whispering in her ear that the climax to her confinement was imminent. It was the following day that he was able to bring us the glad tidings that the *Poellekie* had been responsible for the first known hatching of this species anywhere in Europe. The chick, rich brown in colouring, with two parallel yellow stripes down its back, looked rather like a bumble-bee on stilts. Being an only child, it was ridiculously spoiled by its foster-parents, Cees and the *Poellekie*, offering it endless mealworms and other tidbits. Very soon after this birth, the Malay hen presented us with another egg and before the year was out she laid a third, and all of the chicks were successfully reared.

From time to time we allow the parent birds to incubate and rear their own offspring. The geese and swans are always exemplary parents. Not only do both sexes share the nursery chores, but they are also large enough to protect their eggs from magpies, or other winged raiders, and their young from the hostile attentions of other waterfowl.

Ducks, with very few exceptions, score nought out of ten for parenthood. Father is unlikely to take any interest in his children, who stand little chance of survival in a rowdy, mixed collection. Hen pheasants would normally make devoted mothers, but aviary conditions often preclude natural rearing methods. Only the very smallest mesh of wire netting can contain the chicks and, even if the pen is thus constructed, the cock bird will frequently attack and kill his progeny.

While broody hens or bantams offer the most natural alternative, they too can have their disadvantages. Not infrequently, and not surprisingly, a chicken may take exception to the strange creatures that emerge from her clutch of eggs and squash them, ruthlessly, at birth. Then again, even with the best of husbandry, all poultry are notorious disease carriers. Dora and Dulcie, Peg-leg and the *Poellekie* are all dosed regularly against fowl-pest, parasitic worms and other infections and all look to be in first-class health. There is every likelihood, however, that their tough little bodies have built up an immunity to various diseases to which the more delicate strains of pheasants and waterfowl can easily succumb.

To try and eliminate these risks, many breeders use completely artificial methods of hatching and rearing. Incubators, standard practice now in the commercial poultry industry and for most game farms, are available in a variety of models for ornamental birds. They are expensive, laboursaving and hygenic, but often of dubious efficiency. The embryo in a chicken egg is so strong that it can be subjected to all manner of indignities – excessive storage, overheating, under-heating and so on – and a perfectly sound chick will usually leap out of the shell after the allotted period of twenty-one days. Doctors, I have been told, have even been known to prescribe, as a form of therapeutic exercise for women confined to hospital for long periods, the incubation of a chicken egg between their breasts. I must confess that I have yet to hear of a successful hatching by this method – a lot must depend on both the patience and proportions of the female concerned – but a number of years ago we did unwittingly become involved in one such experiment.

The local policeman's wife was a kindly but neurotic soul. George, her husband, had been transferred to this lawabiding area by a sympathetic police force who realized that much of his time had to be spent looking after Elsie, a native of East Anglia. From time to time he drove her up to the farm, especially during the breeding season, where her greatest joy was to be allowed to fondle and stroke the newest arrivals. They had no children of their own and much of her affection was lavished on their two pet budgerigars and various casualties, such as starlings with broken wings, that George picked up from the roadside on his intermittent patrols through the surrounding countryside. Few survived the gastronomic ordeal of fish fingers, chips and buttered toast and marmalade to which they were subjected, but they would have been unlikely to fare much better had George not rescued them.

One cold and rainy day in March he came alone to the house on his police motorcycle. Elsie, he told me, had slipped a disc and the doctor had ordered her to lie flat on her back until the pain eased. He removed his helmet, scratched his bald head and looked at me with obvious discomfort.

'Oi'm zorry to ask it of you, Zirr,' he said in his rich Devon accent, 'but you 'aven't got no eggs ter spare, 'ave you?'

'Of course you can have some eggs', I replied. 'The chickens aren't laying very well at the moment, but I'm sure we can fix you up with half a dozen. And what about a pot of honey for Elsie?'

Helmet in one hand and honey in the other, he walked with me to the food-shed on the farm. He was an imposing figure of a man, in his late forties I would guess, but not dissimilar in voice and physique to the Guards sergeant-major under whom I had trained. The village respected his authority. There were just eight small bantam eggs on the shelf, so I put two in my pocket for supper that evening and handed him the rest. Shifting uneasily from one leg to the other, he regarded them with some suspicion.

'Be these eggs fertile?' he inquired, looking firmly at his boots.

'Why, er yes, they should be. Hop-along Cassidy's a bit off colour – just going through his annual moult – but, Mole's in good form. But why? Is it important?'

'Well, its like this, Major, my Elsie she read in one of them there women's magazines as 'ow patients in 'ospitals zumtimes try to 'atch an egg while they're laid up. Zeems as it

90

zort of keeps their morale up and gives 'em zummat to do.'

He looked up at me in some apprehension, clearly hoping that no further explanation was necessary.

'George,' I said, struggling hard to keep a straight face, 'I know exactly what you mean.' The strong arm of the law looked relieved. 'I personally believe its just one of those old wives' tales, but if Elsie wants to have a go at hatching a chicken, she won't find much wrong with these eggs. The incubation period's three weeks,' was my parting remark as his motorcycle disappeared down the drive.

It was fortunate that I remembered to relate the incident to Cees, for I was away when the great moment arrived and it was he who had to take on the role of midwife. Almost exactly three weeks later, George and Elsie drove up to the farm in a state of feverish excitement.

'It's hatching, it's hatching! What do I do?' she shouted.

Cees asked to see the egg, whereupon she plunged both hands down her ample cleavage and proudly presented it to him.

'Look!' she said, 'It's beginning to chip. We're soon going to have a little baby.' George, resplendent in his best uniform, bashfully nodded his agreement.

One glance told Cees that the large crack in the egg was in no way attributable to a chick about to hatch. Some sudden jarring movement had fractured the shell. Tactfully, he asked them to wait where they were, explaining that he wanted to take it into the brooder-shed to examine it with the aid of the candler.

Having confirmed that the egg was as clear as a whistle, he sat down on a food-bin and lit his pipe. He had no idea how he was going to deal with this dilemma. Fortunately, inspiration soon came. Moving over to our old incubator, he opened the door and looked at the hatching tray. He was in luck.

When he rejoined George and Elsie, he was holding a newly-born chick in his hands. Elsie, seeing her new infant for the first time, rushed up to take it and immediately immersed it protectively in her bosom.

'Oh, you dear little chick, you darling bird,' she crooned, while the poor creature cheeped pathetically from the Stygian depths. Then, on an impulse, she turned to Cees.

'How has it managed to get dry so quickly?' She asked him.

Lesser mortals would have been floored by this one. Cees, phlegmatic as ever, sucked slowly on his pipe for a moment or two. Then, removing it from his mouth, he pointed the stem at her chest. 'How could anything become damp een such a vonderful, varm oven?'

The incubator from which he had taken the chick was a remarkable machine. During our first breeding season I had bought it in the local market for three pounds and since then it had hatched several thousand birds. I say 'hatched', but it would be more accurate if I were to write 'finished off hatching.' For many years the broody hens have done ninety-five percent of the work, sitting for weeks, sometimes months, on series of eggs of every sort. Only when they were chipped, or almost chipped, did the old paraffin incubator take over.

We have, over the years, tried a variety of more expensive machines but while they could be relied upon to have a near-perfect hatch of any eggs from the hen-house, the results with ornamental pheasant or waterfowl eggs were always disappointing. Our experience has been by no means unique and that is why a great many breeders still prefer the old fashioned method of broodies, or 'cluckers'. Experts will argue for hours on end about egg-turning, wet-bulb readings, dry-bulb readings and ideal temperatures for goose or pheasant eggs, but few people, if any, have come up with a perfect solution. Very recently we have in fact acquired an excellent machine, but even when one gets a good hatch, there can be other problems that do not arise with broodies. The chicks need warmth for the first two or three weeks, and this is normally supplied by electric heating lamps. Unless one has one's own generator, a sudden power cut can cause irreparable damage. Likewise, all young birds benefit from having some form of mother. Broodies not only provide heat, but teach the chicks to feed, protect them from outside danger and exert a degree of parental authority. Pheasant poults, as anyone who has kept them knows to his cost, are extremely prone to feather-pecking, which in turn may lead to cannibalism. Young pheasants with some form of mother are much less addicted to this vice. The family instinct is most highly developed among geese and swans. The young normally remain attached to their parents for at least their first migration and sometimes longer. Their requirement for a mother is exceptionally strong, in complete contrast to ducklings in captivity, who seem perfectly happy being thrown into a nursery pen with others of roughly similar age.

Much has already been written, by Konrad Lorenz and others, on the imprinting habits of goslings. On hatching, these tiny creatures form an immediate bond with the first creature they see that gives them warmth and affection. The heavier breeds of poultry, like light Sussex or Rhode Island reds, are ideally suited to their needs, whereas inanimate pig-lamps are not. It sometimes happens, therefore, that goslings reared in this manner form a fixation on their keepers. Since most human beings love and respond to flattery, the imprinting habit can readily be induced. The trouble is that unless one has limitless time and patience, to say nothing of a very understanding husband or wife, it can easily lead to complications.

The first summer after we were married, Brunhilde objected to three more goslings being introduced to her already large family and Didy suggested that we should rear them ourselves. Three newly hatched bar-headed goslings accordingly took up residence in the house. They were enchanting little balls of animated fluff and followed us wherever we went. There comes a stage, however, with all young waterfowl when their soft, downy plumage begins to be replaced with rudimentary feathers and, to me at any rate, they lose much of their early charm. When they were about a month old Didy had to prepare a dinner party at very short notice. The pandemonium that invariably attends any kind

93

of formal entertaining at Daws Hall is always made worse by one or more dogs, that trip us up while waiting for scraps to fall. On this occasion the addition of six large, webbed feet, scuttering all over the kitchen floor and depositing excessively slippery droppings, did nothing to alleviate the chaos. But they survived and so did we to enjoy an excellent dinner.

The first imprinted gosling that I ever had was a lesser snow. Geese and goslings all live predominantly on grass, and the parents teach their young to graze as soon as they walk off the nest. This little creature, of course, had no-one but me to train it. The first thing I had to do was to look carefully over the wall to see that none of the neighbours was watching; then, lying on my belly, I began nibbling at the lawn with my teeth. The gosling promptly followed suit. Whenever it needed warmth, I popped it inside my shirt. Throughout the day it made the most pathetic peeping noises if abandoned for more than a moment, though darkness fortunately seemed to induce sleep and a cardboard box, old jersey and hot water bottle combined to provide its night nursery. Shortly after it was hatched I rashly decided to take it to church, where I was due to read the lesson. I should perhaps add that I do not make a point of taking birds to church, but, on this occasion, it looked so pathetic when I rushed out of the house I took pity on it and popped it inside my shirt. That it disapproved of a tweed suit, collar and tie as much as the wearer was made abundantly clear to the whole congregation. First it nibbled my tummy-button and then it made a determined and vociferous dash for freedom. Scrambling down the inside of my shirt and over my underpants, it dropped down one trouser-leg and made its way to the centre of the aisle. The completion of the last six verses of the fourth chapter of the *Second Book of Samuel*, with the attention of the entire congregation focused on a two-day old gosling, was an experience I never wish to repeat.

Although bees can be pleasantly disposed towards one person and extremely aggressive to another, this is not

A two-day-old gosling had little competition from the lesson

caused by imprinting. They are, anyway, far too independent, temperamental and strong-willed ever to be subjected to the will of any human being. Some nationalities are by nature more aggressive than others, and Italians – I refer to the bees of course – are invariably foul-tempered. Their reaction to people appears to be dependent on various factors, including the weather, the time of year, and the physical and mental approach of their keeper. They dislike thundery weather, rough handling and certain smells and types of clothing. Knowledgeable bee-keepers only visit their hives when weather conditions are right. They wear white, or light clothing, avoid any sudden movement and, above all, adopt a kindly, yet confident attitude towards the inmates. Any sign of fear is immediately detected and will arouse the bees to anger.

As a child I had often helped the gamekeeper with his bees. First, there was the spring inspection of the hives, usually on a warm day at the end of March, when we checked that the inmates had come through the winter in good heart and were queen-right. Later there were extra brood frames and supers to add, queen cells to pinch out and then, just after harvest, it was time to take the honey. I remember that Cecil never wore any protective clothing and, since I would not have dared to have been thought a coward, I followed his example. In those days there were bee-keepers in every village. It was an inexpensive hobby and, since pesticides were almost unknown, the shelves in most larders held pots of honey, stacked alongside home-made jams and bottled fruits. Now, with bees of my own, I must admit that I do usually wear a bee-suit, veil and gloves, although there have been occasions when I have donned no armour at all. Sometimes I have paid the penalty, but more often than not I have come out unscathed. Reactions to bee-stings vary between individuals. If I am stung on a sensitive area, like the lobe of an ear or close to an eye, it is extremely painful, but generally speaking I am fortunate in finding them no worse than stings from a nettle.

Several summers ago I was staying in the north of England with a friend who had just acquired his first stock, and one afternoon I accompanied him to the local bee-keeping course. Our instructor was a prim and elderly spinster. Her head and neck were covered with a gauze veil, but she was wearing the thinnest of cotton frocks, sandals, and no gloves or stockings.

It was a sultry day; dark clouds were beginning to gather on the horizon. The six immaculate white hives stood in the garden of the president of the local bee-keeping association and their height, almost two metres from the ground, was evidence both of his skill and the labours of many thousands of bees. Clad like the dozen or so other students in full regalia, I assisted by operating the smoker. Each hive was dismantled down to the two lower boxes containing brood chambers and from these our instructor removed every frame in turn, holding them up for our inspection. The purpose of the exercise was to teach us to identify and remove queen cells which, if allowed to hatch, would lead to the loss of bees through swarming.

Watching her work through the hives was an education in itself. Every movement was slow and deliberate and one could not but sense the empathy between her and the bees. They crawled all over her bare arms, they sat on her fingers and all the while a quiet, contented humming noise emanated from the hives. As she reached the sixth and final hive, there was a distant peel of thunder and darkening clouds scurried across the sky.

The reaction of the bees was instantaneous and a sudden warning noise came out of the hive. Looking down into it, I could see a throng of angry insects, massing for attack.

'Quick, more smoke,' she said.

I puffed hard with the smoker and it soon began to have the desired effect. The indignant buzzing gradually subsided. One bee, however, had got inside my veil and I felt a sharp stab at the back of my neck. Some of the other students, I noticed, were having similar problems and one young girl grabbed her bosom and fled to the privacy of a nearby hedgerow.

'I think,' announced our instructor in a calm and matter-of-fact voice, 'that we'll call it a day.'

As she spoke I saw three or four bees bury their poisoned darts in her bare wrists. She did not flinch at all, but carried on with the work of reassembling the hive, pausing only to brush them off as though they were particles of offending dust. Then I saw a new danger approaching. There were quite a lot of bees in the grass and several of these now launched a new attack up our legs. To those of us who were guarded by gumboots and bee-suits they presented no problem; our instructor alone was vulnerable. All eyes were fixed on two bees which had now reached her left knee and were continuing their ascent in a determined fashion. Seconds later they had disappeared from view under the hem of her cotton dress and two more started their upward march on her right leg.

Seizing the smoker from on top of the hive, I directed it onto the cluster of bees around her sandalled feet and they quickly dispersed. The second wave, however, was by now at her knees and I thought it tactful to refrain from blowing hot smoke up her dress. A hush descended on the students as we waited for her reaction. I noticed that the young lady with the bee in her bosom had now rejoined us and, somewhat pink in the face, was gazing in open-mouthed astonishment at our instructor's calm and unruffled expression.

We had not long to wait. There was a sudden tensing of her body and she cast her eyes heavenwards. Then, her lips parted and four muffled squeaks came forth, followed by what sounded remarkably like a long drawn out, ecstatic moan of pleasure.

With our own bees, each year brings a varying harvest. There is no shortage of pollen and nectar on the farm. Even on warm days in February and March, the heads of Cees's early spring bulbs are smothered with foraging bees. Later, sycamore and horse chestnut trees, dandelions and clover, brambles, buddleia and a host of wild flowers and garden plants are alive with myriads of buzzing insects. Always, it seems that the burgeoning hives will produce a bumper crop, but then, in July, when the avenue of lime trees is in flower and the honey flow has reached its peak, we will invariably be plagued by swarms. It is usually about midday that we hear a distant droning noise and then a great cloud of bees, with precious honey on board, will fly over the pheasant aviaries and disappear into the distance. Sometimes we manage to retrieve them, but all too often they settle in some inaccessible place, where they live for a short while before perishing from cold and starvation. It says little for my bee-keeping ability, but despite these losses there never seems to be any shortage of honey for ourselves and our friends.

We take the crop during the children's summer holidays. Each of us has his or her own job to do and for forty-eight hours everything in the kitchen, from the floor to the walls, and occasionally the ceiling, is smothered in honey. Even Fuzzy, perched on her beam, managed to get covered with sticky honeycomb during the summer that she spent with us as a fledgling.

My task is to collect the honey from the hives. The supers containing capped frames are loaded into the car and then, dressed like a traveller to outer space, I drive them down to the back door. There Cees takes over and stacks the boxes close to the kitchen sink, where Didy is boiling up a constant supply of hot water for easing the bread-knife through the outer cappings. As soon as the wax has been removed and placed in an earthenware bowl, the honey starts to flow. Four frames at a time are placed in the extractor, where Cees's muscles come into play. The ancient machine rattles and clatters as he turns the wheel at a furious speed. The children, meanwhile, are busy straining, decanting and sticking labels onto jars and honey onto themselves. From time to time we all pause, wipe sweat and honey from our faces and plunge long spoons into the various jugs and containers for further samples of the golden and glorious liquid.

99

Tim was with us one August, when we had an exceptionally heavy crop.

'Wot about brewing up a spot of mead?' he suggested.

'What's mead?' chorused the children.

'Lovely, lovely, alcoholic honey.' Tim licked his lips in anticipation.

'Ugh,' said Katrina.

'Can you get *very* drunk on it?' asked Hugh.

Tim explained how it was made, 'You boil up honey, cinnamon, cloves, a little tea and the rind from lemons and oranges. Then you allow the mixture to cool and add some yeast. The only trouble,' he added wistfully, 'is that you're meant to leave the bottles for two years before drinking it.'

Didy reluctantly produced a colossal preserving pan that was normally reserved for making jam. 'If you ruin this, I'll throttle you,' she announced. And Tim set about pouring in all the ingredients. Ambrosial, aromatic smells wafted through all the downstairs rooms and, several weeks later, after the various stages of fermentation were completed, he strained the mead into close on two dozen wine bottles. (We would have had several more but for the temptation to carry out frequent tastings.) While Tim was scrubbing the utensils that we had used, I carefully inserted corks and carried the bottles down to the cellar, where I laid them on their sides.

Shortly after this we went up to Scotland on holiday. In the excitement of two of the children catching their first trout, to say nothing of some splendid salmon fishing and literally hundreds of mackerel caught in the sea off Helmsdale, the nectar of the Gods was soon forgotten. It was Angus who first went down to the cellar on our return. 'I must check whether anyone has stolen my port,' is invariably his first remark on coming into the house after any absence. He came back up the steps looking rather surprised. 'Daddy, there's a horrible mess all over the cellar floor, but my twelve bottles of port are still all right.'

Mouthing some uncharitable comments about the case of Crofts '60 that he had been given ten years previously as a christening present, I rushed down the steps. Three-quarters of the bottles had blown their corks and the cellar floor was awash with mead. Hastening to the far end where the bottles were stored, I slipped on the well lubricated flagstones.

'Mind the port!' came Angus's shrill voice.

As I landed flat on my back, another bottle exploded.

With Angus's help I recorked the few survivors, this time standing them upright to allow the remaining bubbles to escape.

For Christmas that year, Angus gave me an instruction manual on home-made wines and I determined to make amends. One of the earliest and easiest of wines for beginners, the book told me, was dandelion. I was particularly relieved to read that it could be drunk as little as three months after bottling, although apparently it became increasingly potent the longer it was left.

Early the following spring, the two-acre poplar field below the bottom pond was bright yellow with flowering dandelions. Later, in the same area, their taller cousins, the hawkweeds would blossom in profusion. Both have for centuries been used, not only for country wines, but for salads and herbal remedies. 'The juice of the hawkweed taken in wine,' says an old writer, 'or the decoction drank, helpeth the jaundice, although of long continuance, if drank night and morning.' It was also one of the plants used by alchemists, for he goes on to say that 'The moon owns this herbe also, and though authors cry out upon alchemists for attempting to fix quicksilver by this herbe and Moonwort, a Roman would not have judged a thing by success; if it be fixed at all, it is fixed by lunar influence.'

Gathering the ingredients was a more laborious process than I had anticipated. All the petals had to be separated from the tough outer calyx, and it took the best part of a day to fill a couple of buckets with the yellow florets. On my return to the house, I weighed the contents, tipped them into an earthenware crock and added the recommended amount of boiling water. They emitted a pungent and rather acrid

101

odour, which I trusted would bear no resemblance to the final bouquet.

The crock was placed in the large, south-facing window of the children's playroom and every morning when I came down to breakfast I gave the mixture a vigorous stir. The warm spring weather soon activated fermentation and an encouraging hubble-bubble began. At the end of a week I followed the instructions and strained off and discarded all the froth and petals. Didy's store-cupboard was raided for lemons, raisins and brown sugar, which were added to the brew, and finally I stirred in some yeast. When I next walked into the room, I thought the plumbing had gone wrong. The crock resembled a witch's cauldron.

Three months to the day after bottling what the French very aptly term *pissenlit*, I brought up the first bottle from the cellar. Didy was away staying with her parents that night; my dinner was in the oven, my favourite television programme was on, so the stage was set for a quiet but hedonistic evening. My only concern was whether the *château*-bottled dandelion would come up to expectations.

I poured myself a tumblerful and held it up to the light. It was crystal-clear and the colour of palest amber. I sniffed it, a little suspiciously at first, and my nostrils inhaled a soft but subtle fragrance, redolent of wild flowers and freshly mown spring pastures. The first glass slipped down very nicely. I fetched my dinner from the kitchen, switched on the television and settled down in a comfortable armchair with the bottle on the table beside me.

About an hour later, the telephone rang. As I got up to answer it, I was aware that my footsteps were far from steady. This was nothing, however, compared to my voice when I tried to speak.

An enormously wealthy customer of ours was on the line, a man who could normally be relied on to contribute single-handed to around forty per cent of our gross annual turnover. Having been to visit us on several occasions, I knew that he was a strict teetotaller.

102

'Any rare waterfowl for sale?' He demanded.

I gargled something quite incomprehensible into the mouthpiece. There was a pause, followed by a polite cough at the other end.

'I say, old chap, are you feeling all right?' He enquired with what I thought was very commendable solicitude.

I swallowed hard, then opened my mouth and attempted to reply. Only the fumes of the *pissenlit* emerged. For God's sake, I thought, pull yourself together. Get something out and keep it brief.

'Are you still there?' Asked our chief benefactor.

'Thank you, I'm fine,' seemed a suitably short and ambiguous reply and I mouthed it once to myself before trying it aloud. What came out bore very little resemblance to what was intended.

Again, a pause at the other end before he patiently repeated his original enquiry.

Fumbling among the papers on my desk, I succeeded in locating a copy of our current list of birds for sale. Precious little scope for monosyllabism here I realized to my consternation. White-winged wood ducks and Argentinian shovellers are a mouthful at the best of times and I gave an involuntary little shudder. I heard myself say something about 'zhizhingzhooders', before breaking off in acute embarrassment.

'This line's awfully bad,' he remarked a little testily. 'Can you hear *me* all right?'

Straining my battered faculties to the utmost, I made one final and supreme attempt at vocal coherency. 'No,' I replied and experienced a brief moment of pride at the clarity of my enunciation.

'I'll try to get a better line and call you back,' he said and I hung up the receiver.

As I inched my way up the staircase, I heard the telephone ring once more. By the time I had succeeded in negotiating the top landing and opening the bedroom door, the noise had thankfully ceased.

Chapter Six

'My life is a bore in this nasty pond,
And I long to go out in the world beyond!'
The Duck and the Kangaroo – Edward Lear

We never actually met the Lady with the Mallard.

It was one evening in April that she first rang up. 'Is that the bird breeders?' she enquired and I dutifully acknowledged our identity. 'Well, you see, it's like this. A mallard has come into my garden and laid three eggs and I don't know what to do with them.'

A number of possible answers flashed through my mind, but I confined myself to enquiring politely whether the duck in question had made a nest.

'Well, it sort of has and it sort of hasn't,' she replied.

'Oh, I see.'

'Actually, its made three nests,' she continued, 'but all in different places. The last one's on my back doorstep.'

'How very complicated.'

'Yes, it is, isn't it? And I don't know what to do with the eggs.'

We seemed to be getting nowhere, so I took a deep breath. 'Now then, let's start at the beginning. Where did she lay her first egg?'

'In the flower bed. It was a lovely nest, but I was worried about passion.'

'Passion?' I wondered if I had heard her correctly.

'Passion's my poodle.' What an extraordinary name for a dog, I thought. She must have sensed my perplexity, for she continued: 'Yes, it is a rather funny name. Shall I tell you why I called him Passion?'

I could see that this was going to be a lengthy telephone call, but as I had nothing particular to do, and I was also rather intrigued, I said in my most affable tone of voice, 'Please do.'

'Well, when he was a puppy, he used to spend his pennies on the floor of the lounge . . .'

'Not all that unusual for puppies,' I interjected.

'Oh, you keep dogs too, do you?' I grunted in a non-committal sort of way, anxious to avoid too many further distractions. 'Now then, where was I?'

'Passion,' I prompted.

'Oh yes, when he was about eight weeks old I gradually began to get him house-trained. And where outside do you think he spent his first penny?'

'On the grass?'

'No, silly-billy! Try again.'

'Against a tree?'

'Nearly right. It was against the passion flower that grows up the side of the house. Mine's about twelve years old now and it flowers every year. Anyway, that's how my little doggie got his name. And as he always spends his pennies in the same place and I didn't want him to disturb the mallard, I took the egg away and put it in the hedge at the end of the garden.'

'Ah.'

'Well, anyway, the next day I saw the mallard going into the hedge and that's where she laid her second egg.'

'Good.'

'It wasn't good at all, because she laid it about ten yards away from where I put the first one, right at the end of the hedge where I've seen the neighbours' cat go. I didn't want any accident to happen, so I put the second egg with the first one. That was yesterday and today she laid an egg . . .'

'On your doorstep?', I said, quick as a flash. I knew I was onto a winner this time.

'Exactly. Now you've got the picture.'

Realizing that the time had come for the oracle to speak, I

explained that the best thing she could do was to join the third egg up with the other two and wait to see where number four would be deposited. (There was every likelihood, I felt, of the duck deserting her garden for a more salubrious nesting area, but politely refrained from saying so). Then, I told her, so long as it was in a sensible nesting area, she should leave the poor bird alone and let nature take its course. 'I'm sure the duck will choose a nice nesting site,' I added, 'and then, after she has laid four or five eggs in it, you can join up the other three with them. The incubation period is twenty-eight days.'

April gave place to May and the scent of blossom hung on the air. The early cherries were over now, but close to the main pond the fragrant white flowers of cherry laurels, much loved by the bees, hung low over the water's edge. Blackthorn blossomed in the hedgerows, where the monotonous call of the male cuckoos echoed over the farm until late into the evening. The females by now were avidly studying the nesting activities of reed warblers, dunnocks and pied wagtails, prior to depositing their monstrous eggs. Although only one would be laid in each fragile bower, the hen cuckoo will often lay as many as twelve or thirteen eggs in a year, almost invariably selecting a nest of the same species as that by which she was fostered.

Didy next got involved with our unseen friend. 'Oh, hello, it's the Lady with the Mallard,' she announced on the telephone and then went on to recount how, against all odds, the duck had eventually settled for the artificial nesting site in the hedgerow. Twelve green eggs had been laid.

'Good,' said Didy.

'Well, it's sort of good and it isn't good.'

'Oh?'

'Well, you see, I don't think there are any babies in the eggs. Your husband said they would take four weeks to hatch and today's the twenty-eighth day.'

'But, it is only two or three weeks at the most since you first rang up.'

106

'I know, silly girl, but I wrote down all the dates in my diary. The first egg was laid on Passion's birthday.'

'I'm not quite with you.'

'What, about Passion? He's my poodle.'

'Yes, I know,' said Didy. There was a trace of weariness in her voice. Sitting on the opposite side of the large partners' desk in the study, I was relieved that I was being spared a second round. Sensing Didy's needs, I walked over to the drinks tray and poured her a large glass of sherry.

'Now then, my diary's right here, Passion's birthday is on the fourteenth of April and today's the twelfth of May.'

'When was the last egg laid?' Didy took a gulp of sherry and raised her eyes to the ceiling as she waited for the reply.

'Hang on. Yes, its here. The first of this month.'

'Well, they're due to hatch around the twenty-eighth or twenty-ninth.'

'That wasn't what your husband said.'

Didy patiently explained that a mother duck will lay her eggs at one or two day intervals and that, although she will spend quite a large part of the day sitting on the nest, no incubation will start until the clutch is complete. 'So you see, there's another fortnight to go before any ducklings are due to come out.'

'Ah, now I understand. By the way, you don't mind me asking you all these questions, do you?'

'Of course not. That's what we're here for.' I scowled disapprovingly as she went on: 'Just give us a ring any time that you think we can be of assistance.'

She did, and again it was Didy who answered the telephone. We were already late for an appointment with the dentist and I was hovering impatiently by the study door, the pain from a broken tooth getting worse every minute.

After the usual introduction, she explained that she was very worried about two of the eggs which the mallard had rolled out of the nest. 'The bird doesn't seem to want to sit on them,' she said, 'and they look a horrible blotchy colour. I don't know what to do with them.'

'I could tell her what to bloody well do with them,' I said. 'Come on, we're late.'

'Ssh,' said Didy, quickly putting her hand over the mouth-piece and looking angrily in my direction. Then, in her normal, dulcet tones; 'I think you'll find that the duck knows that those two are addled and that's why she has hoofed them out. Look, I'm awfully sorry to interrupt you, but we're . . .'

'Late,' I shouted.

A week passed before we heard from her again. This time, it was my turn.

'Hello, it's the Lady with the Mallard here.'

'Oh, yes,' I said without much enthusiasm. 'How's it all going? Any ducklings?' I realized it must be about D-Day.

'Well, yes and no.' I might have guessed that that would be her answer.

'What, some are off, are they?' I asked.

'Exactly. I saw three little babies sitting close to her in the hedge this morning, just after breakfast, and they still haven't had anything to eat. Do you think I should give them some bread and milk in Passion's dinner bowl?'

'No, I really don't think that's necessary,' I told her. 'It's very important at this stage that you don't disturb her. She knows exactly what to do and I think you'll find that tomorrow, when the rest of them are hatched and dry, she'll take them off the nest together to a place where they can eat and drink.'

'Oh, but that's cruel! The first poor little mites will be dead from starvation by then.'

'No, they won't,' I said. 'Nature sees to it that they have a good meal from the remains of the egg and they don't need anything else for up to forty-eight hours.'

'Is that so?'

I assured her that it was.

Every time that the telephone rang the next day, Didy and I raced each other to say 'feigns' and the last one, of course, had to take the call. We were certain that she would ring us up sometime during the day, but we were wrong.

The last couple of weeks in May saw signs of feverish activity everywhere on the farm. Many of the summer migrants had by now got young in the nest and hundreds of extra mouths waited impatiently to be fed. All day long, chiffchaffs and willow warblers, spotted flycatchers and whitethroats, blackcaps, sandpipers and hosts of other visitors from foreign shores toiled to bring food to their fledglings. Along the river, great flattened banks of reeds provided nesting sites for numerous moorhens and there, too, the tufted ducks were sitting tight on their dark green eggs. Solitary herons flew lazily along the valley and sudden flashes of bright, metallic blue announced the presence of one of our resident pairs of kingfishers.

Within our four acre, fox-proof fence, the garden birds were equally busy and there, protected from cats and other vermin, tiny creatures, too young to fly, lived in perfect safety. Every spring and summer the big window in the brooder-shed had to be left open in all weathers, to enable the swallows to fly in and out, and, close to where we kept the food-bins, a blackbird nested in one of Cees's outsize clogs.

One morning at the end of the month Cees came into the kitchen with a worried look on his face.

'Trouble?' we asked.

'No, all is vell, but there are several telephone messages that I took vile you were out last night. I haf got an order for black swans from a zoo een Scotland, some man from Belgium is coming here tomorrow afternoon to see ze pheasants and then, just as I vas going to bed, a funny voman rang up.'

'Oh, what did she want?'

'Vell, I don't quite know. She sounded a leetle bit strange in ze head.'

Didy and I exchanged glances. 'She didn't by any chance want advice over a family of mallard, did she?' I asked.

'She did say something about a mallard to begin with, but then she started talking in a funny vay about her babies. Anyvay, she asked me to give you a message.

Putting his pipe and corduroy Leninist cap down on the kitchen table, he fumbled in his trouser pockets and handed me a scrap of paper. It read as follows: 'My Passion's frightened the babies away.'

Not long after this, while Tim was having a painting and vermin catching sojourn at Daws Hall, another woman rang up and told me that a strange bird had flown into her kitchen, where it was demolishing the cat's food. We began to believe that the local countryside was populated by nothing but eccentric, bird-mad females.

'Go on, Tim', I said wearily. 'Your turn now.'

When he returned an hour later in the Landrover, we could not believe our eyes. There, sitting happily on his shoulder, was Fuzzy. She had been away for six months and yet, from her behaviour, she might never have left us. How had she survived? Had some kind family adopted her? We shall probably never know all the answers, but it seemed certain to us, and Tim in particular, that she could not have lived all that time without human assistance. The young kestrel, which we had released with high hopes of being able to fend for herself, was clearly still imprinted on human beings.

'Well, Tim, where are you going to put her now?' asked Didy. From the tone of her voice, it was clear that she was not exactly offering the kitchen as a continued depository for raptorial defecations.

At that moment Fuzzy, excited by all the sudden attention, cocked her tail and slurped all over Tim's Norwegian jersey.

'Tim, there's only one answer,' I said. 'You know the two empty aviaries behind the brooder-shed? They've got plenty of room and lots of high perches and I really think we ought to put her in one of them, anyway for the time being. Put her in the one that she occupied during Aunt Isabel's visit.' I added as an afterthought.

Tim reluctantly agreed. After carrying Fuzzy to the aviary, he went off with his ·22 to get her dinner.

It was not an entirely happy arrangement. Whenever she heard the sound of human voices, Fuzzy set up an incessant mewing which only ceased when one of us went into her aviary and scratched the top of her head. As soon as we left, this pathetic noise started once more. We were faced with a difficult problem and one that was of our own making. The cuddly fledgling, on which we had lavished so much love and attention the previous year, had now become a creature that belonged to neither world. It was her solitary life that worried me particularly and I discussed with Tim the possibility of acquiring a mate for her.

'Could be a bit dodgy,' he said and went on to explain that not infrequently an imprinted female will turn against the much smaller cock bird and kill him.

Autumn came and the menagerie on the farm gradually decreased as we sold the young birds that we had bred during the season. Most of them went to private breeders in Britain and overseas, while others went to zoos and wildlife parks. The summer migrants, too, began to wing their way to distant shores, leaving a damp stillness in the thickets of bramble, hazel and hawthorn. There the ripening berries would shortly provide winter food for great flocks of fieldfares and redwings, while the colder weather would also bring in snipe and the occasional woodcock and golden plover.

In November we had a weekend visit from some friends who kept a variety of feathered pets at their home in Hampshire. Philip, the third oldest of the five children, already knew far more about the ways of nature than I did when I was twice his age. Among other creatures he had a barn owl and several kestrels, most of which were casualties found on the roads. The hawks he trained to the lure and every day, when he came home from school, he exercised them in the fields around their house.

One day, while his mother was entertaining the local bishop to a glass of sherry, Philip rushed into the house.

'Quick, Mummy, come and help! Hermes is being attacked by a wild kestrel.'

Together they raced into the garden, followed by Bishop Rudgard, and saw the two birds locked in combat under the beech trees. Philip donned his leather gauntlet and tried to separate them, but the wild kestrel clung on. When they were finally parted, it was clear that Hermes was the victor – his aggressor was bleeding from several deep scratches.

Being a doctor's wife and trained nurse to boot, Philip's mother was well qualified to deal with the casualty. 'Bring it into the house, darling, and I'll disinfect the wounds,' she said.

For several days the young male looked extremely sorry for himself, but gradually a combination of gentle handling by Philip and professional nursing from his parents had their effect and the bird recovered. By then, of course, he and the family were all mutually infatuated, so he took up residence with the other tame hawks and was duly christened Rudgard in honour of His Grace.

During the weekend we discussed Fuzzy's future and Philip's father suggested that perhaps Rudgard could come and share her abode. It was clear, however, that young Philip, aged ten and a half, had his reservations.

'I *might* agree to part with Rudgard,' he announced in an enormously solemn voice, 'but I just wonder whether Major Grahame *really* knows how to look after hawks.'

Much to everyone's amusement I was subjected to a barrage of searching questions on essential vitamins, the design of nest boxes and optimum daily weight of food for a young tiercel at different seasons of the year. All of these I endeavoured to answer to the best of my ability, but my ignorance on the captive management of kestrels must have been blatantly apparent. Having put me right, in the politest possible way, on various points, Philip finally announced his verdict.

'I think I might agree to Rudgard coming here on loan, but I should be *dreadfully* upset if anything happened to him.'

Never had such a burden been placed on my shoulders.

Rudgard duly arrived with a set of hand-made jesses, but I was far too frightened to risk trying my hand at falconry and concentrated all my efforts at keeping him alive and confined.

On Philip's advice, we placed him in an adjoining pen to that of Fuzzy and it was fortunate indeed that we kept them apart. Whenever Rudgard came anywhere near the wire netting barrier that separated them, she would fly at him with talons poised for attack, screeching insults at her bridegroom to be. It seemed unlikely that we should ever be able to put them sufficiently close to one another for the marriage to be consummated. As Christmas approached they remained in their separate aviaries.

For several winters we had had an extra harvest to that of the birds. The Christmas trees that had been planted shortly after I bought Daws Hall had reached a marketable size after three or four years. In the early days, Cees and I had struggled and toiled in icy weather, digging them out for the local shops or sending them up to London. At first it had hardly been a gainful pastime. Not only did it seem that the only people who failed to make a reasonable profit were the growers but we were also, on reflection, far too honest about the quality of trees that we sold. Anything that did not have an immaculate leader or was at all lacking in symmetry was discarded and subsequently burnt. Then, very belatedly, we began to realize the possibilities of allowing people to dig their own trees. Smart signboards were put out on the road and Sundays in early December saw the arrival of hordes of gum-booted families, armed with spades, shovels, forks and gardening gloves.

'What sort of size Christmas tree would you like?' We would ask and, almost invariably, they would hold out their arms to indicate one of the smallest ones that we had. Some even wanted a sort of bonsai Norway spruce for putting in a pot on the living room table. We would accordingly direct them to the appropriate part of the field and sit at the seat of custom, devouring the Sunday newspapers while waiting for

113

trees and cash to return.

The trees, by then, ranged from four to fourteen feet in height and the customers' declared aim, in almost every case, was to dig up small trees with roots intact, which could be subsequently replanted in their gardens. Polythene bags and bales of string were often brought along for wrapping their nether regions, while mum and the children were all set to enjoy themselves and act as willing helpers.

From time to time one of us would stroll up to the field to watch the work in progress. It was an interesting study in human psychology and more often than not resulted in a supreme test of father's virility on a Sunday morning.

It took a little time for him to locate the tree of his choice – invariably a small specimen, often hopelessly disfigured, in the nearest part of the field. Just as his spade was poised, there would be a shrill cry from the middle of the plantation. The children, red and blue anoraks flapping in the breeze, had found a tree that was ideally suited for a church or market square.

'Here, Dad! Come and look, we've found a real smasher,' their voices would echo across the field.

The parents would eventually locate their offspring among the sea of green conifers and the new specimen would be submitted to a critical examination.

'Well, it would look ever so nice,' mother would declare, oblivious to the fact that the ceiling of their lounge barely topped the middle branches.

'Go on with you, Norah, we don't live in a blooming palace.'

The children by then had scampered off to the furthest area and once more their shrill voices could be heard. Mother and father trundled off again, dragging their tools through the long grass.

'Please, Dad, this one,' – 'No, this one,' – 'No, this one,' their voices would cry.

Eventually, mother and children would settle for a Christmas tree that was at least twice the size of that which was originally intended. Only father had his doubts.

'You want a bloody bull-dozer to get the roots of that one up,' he would say. 'Anyway, I want to get back to the telly.'

'Oh, come on Sid! Christmas only comes once a year.'

'Yes, come on Daddy! We'll help you,' chorused the children.

Grunting some incorrigible blasphemy, father would remove his jacket and roll up his sleeves. Robins and blackbirds gathered for the impending feast. Twenty minutes of intensive hacking at the frosty ground did little to impair the health of the tree. The birds looked intensely disappointed.

'Go on, Sid! You used to be ever so strong.'

Red in the face, father flexed his muscles, raised the spade and brought it down at the base of the tree with all the force he could muster. There was a loud crack as the handle snapped in two.

'Oh, Dad! Look what you've done now!'

'If you'd spent a few more weekends in the garden, you'd be in practice for this sort of work,' his wife would chide.

'Bloody tools! They don't know how to make them these days. When I was a lad . . .'

We kept a couple of all-metal spades in reserve for such eventualities and father would soon be at work once more with a borrowed implement.

Sometimes it was as much as two hours from the time of arrival that an apoplectic male would stagger back to the house, dragging his lacerated trophy behind him. And the most remarkable thing of all was that the same families came back year after year.

It was a good couple of months after Christmas before there was any change in Fuzzy's attitude towards her intended spouse. Rudgard gradually became a little less timid and by early spring they appeared to be coexisting quite happily in their adjacent aviaries. Both looked extremely well and there was a wonderful blue-grey sheen on the head of our borrowed cock. Tim hung up in Fuzzy's pen a deep nest-box, made out of planks of timber, and it was not

115

long before she started to investigate the inside through the round aperture close to the top. The moment seemed to have come to open the dividing door and let them together, but after much discussion with Cees and Tim we all decided it was safest to delegate the decision.

When I telephoned him during the weekend, Philip listened attentively to my progress report.

'Wild kestrels normally nest in the second half of April,' he told me. 'So any good female should be ready to lay in a couple of weeks time.'

'Fuzzy's an excellent female and she looks in marvellous condition,' I said, leaping to the defence of our pet hawk.

There was a trace of juvenile throat clearing on the other end of the line, as though he was not quite sure how to proceed.

'What's the matter, Philip? Don't you think we've got a chance of breeding from them?'

'Well, um, Rudgard's a good bird . . .'

'And Fuzzy?'

'Well, that's the trouble,' he said. 'She's too, er, humanized. You know, all that spoiling and so on.'

'Oh, I see.'

'I say, you don't mind me criticizing your female, do you?'

'Not at all,' I replied quite untruthfully. Actually, I felt rather hurt. Tim, who was standing beside the telephone, looked thoroughly put out.

'The only hope,' Philip continued in a confident tone of voice, 'is to spend as little time with them as possible. Just go in very quickly once a day and give each of them one dead, day old chick.'

'One? But I always give them four, two each.'

'Gross overfeeding,' proclaimed the expert. 'Just give them one each. I should put them together straight away and then Fuzzy just *might* get sort of unimprinted and go to nest.'

'Ah, so you mean I have your permission to risk letting your absolutely spiffing male be slaughtered by our perfectly useless female?'

116

He laughed, a trifle nervously, I thought. 'Well, I don't think it's very likely, but I should be *jolly* angry if it did happen.'

Being a coward by nature, I waited for a couple of days, when I knew we should be staying with friends, before instructing Cees to open the vital door. As it turned out, all was well. Fuzzy laid a clutch of four eggs, but through no fault of her's they were not fertile. Philip reluctantly agreed that it was Rudgard's virility that was suspect. And so the birds have remained for the last two years. Perhaps, one day, Philip will come up with a cure for his delightful, but impotent kestrel.

Though we never had to deal with any wounds or ailments with either of the two kestrels, there were periodic casualties among our other birds. In the early days we used to call for the vet on the slightest pretence, but as time went by and his monthly bills soared to astronomical heights, we began to carry out simple treatments and operations ourselves. To us, the most depressing aspects were our inability (and indeed the vet's) to diagnose many of the complaints sufficiently early and, worse still, the lack of any will to live by most of our patients. With sanded pheasant aviaries, sparrow-proof wire netting and regular prophylactic treatment against worms, coccidiosis, fowl pest and so on, we were automatically reducing to a bare minimum the incidence of the commoner complaints. Obscure diseases of the liver, heart and respiratory system were difficult to diagnose and often impossible to cure. The pheasants were the main problem, for the waterfowl generally seemed to have a much stronger resistance to diseases and seldom tried to kill one another. Breeds of known aggressive temperament – the black swans, certain geese and the shelduck – were always kept in individual pens and displays of territorial aggression by the other waterfowl were usually more comical than dangerous. Our quartet of fulvous whistling ducks, whom we christened the 'bovver boys', were a typical example. Throughout the spring and summer months the tawny mob went on the

117

rampage, rotting up any happy marriage that they could and then, like cuckoos, depositing odd eggs at random in the nests of other ducks.

I have already referred to the murderous assaults that many pheasants will launch on their mates during the breeding season and the cannibalism which can sometimes occur in rearing pens. It was casualties from such instances that were subjected to our do-it-yourself veterinary surgery. Vets, when performing such operations always produce an impressive array of equipment – curved forceps, special suturing thread and syringes loaded with local anaesthetic – and one pays through the nose for their professional expertise. Having watched our own vet at work on a number of occasions, Cees and I decided that we could perhaps save a bit on the farm expenses. Didy's dressing table was raided for nail-scissors and eyebrow tweezers and her sewing box for needle and thread, while a supply of antibiotics that we kept in a cupboard in the foodshed completed our equipment. It took a little while to perfect the special knot that is used for tying the thread, but thereafter we became fairly proficient. All our patients, some with pink cotton on the scalps, others with green or yellow, lived to tell the tale. After completing each operation, we would dust the wound with a disinfectant powder and finally, for good measure, give the bird an intramuscular antibiotic injection. It was interesting to see that Cees, who would turn green and pass out any time that his own anatomy was threatened with a hypodermic syringe, had no qualms at all about thrusting the weapon into some small and defenceless bird.

The biggest risk was not, surprisingly, from scissors or scalpel piercing some vital organ, nor from post-operative infection, but from shock induced by capture and handling. Many birds are extremely susceptible to stress. From the moment that one of us advanced into the aviary with the trout landing net, there was always a danger that the bird would drop down dead from a heart attack. On the few occasions that this has happened we have threatened to convert our seventy odd aviaries to foreign finches, monkeys or some other more accommodating creature.

Even when we succeed in identifying a particular complaint, it is often not easy for the vet to know what to prescribe. Farm animals, race horses and poultry have volumes of research devoted to their ailments, but no-one seems to have had the inclination to study vitamin deficiencies in blood pheasants or leukosis in pygmy geese. The reason, of course, is that the captive population of so many of the birds that we keep is so small as to preclude any detailed research. Having found what appears to be the appropriate drug, it is as likely as not that the dosage listed on the outside of the packet will tell one that a brood mare requires a 10cc oral injection, or that small breeds (of dogs) require half a capsule with their dinner every day for a week. To translate these measurements into the quantities required by a duckling weighing approximately 140 grams requires the arithmetical genius of an Einstein.

Similar problems apply to nutrition. It is not difficult to keep the majority of our adult stock alive, but to get them into perfect breeding condition and to cater for the varying requirements of young birds, many of which have a highly specialized diet in the wild, is no easy task. Apart from various cereals, we use a variety of compound rations that are manufactured for turkeys. This we have chosen in preference to poultry pellets on account of the higher percentage of protein contained. It is not the complete answer, of course, since some of our birds require an exceptionally high level of protein, while others do not, and the feeding habits of a few species in the wild state are simply not known. Inevitably we have to carry out a certain amount of experimentation, though this has to be limited by the amount and value of our stock. And it is not just a problem of finding the best form of food either, for quantities are equally important. Many people, worried that their birds will die from starvation, give them a daily ration that is sufficient to maintain an ostrich or cassowary for a week. The result is that the rat population

119

has a feast and their valuable geese or pheasants become far too fat to breed.

Obesity is not the only cause of infertile eggs or failure to lay. Disturbance and inbreeding are others. Heartened by the success that hormone injections had had on our male blue eared pheasant, we decided to try the same experiment on our Edwards's pheasants. The distribution of this species in the wild is, so far as is known, confined to a small forested area of Vietnam. Hostilities there may well have exterminated it now in the wild state. The cock bird is one of the most beautiful of all pheasants: predominantly midnight blue with traces of metallic green, it has bright, scarlet wattles and a white crest. Virtually nothing is known of their natural habits, and it was not until 1895 that the breed was first discovered by a French missionary in the mountains of the interior of Quangtri Province. For almost thirty years the skins of three males and one female, in the Paris Museum, were all that was known to science. Then, in 1923, Jean Delacour doyen of ornithologists, collected and brought to his home in France four cocks and three hens, and a few more were imported a little later. All captive stock in the world today are descended from these birds. Without any further infusion of fresh blood, the Edwards's pheasants in collection have begun to show markedly degenerative symptoms – a diminution of the white crests in the cocks, infertility deformed offspring and a preponderance of males hatched.

In 1974 our four pairs had laid a total of seventy-four eggs and from these two solitary cock birds were hatched and reared. Aviculturists in other countries were experiencing similar problems.

'I theenk the cocks could do with a jab,' Cees announced early the following spring and a jab they received, three weeks before the hens were due to lay.

We decided, as an experiment, to do the injections again a fortnight later, hoping that extra libido would result. We were, we knew, taking a risk, not only in handling the birds but also in repeating the treatment, which might well upset

120

their whole behaviour and metabolism.

When the time came to administer the second dose, the operation did not go entirely according to plan. I was carrying out the injections single-handed, and had just completed two out of the four, when I was summoned to the house to answer a long distance telephone call. Another quarter of an hour and it would be dark, and as I was passing through the garden I saw that Cees had just finished weeding the herbaceous border.

'Here,' I said, handing him the syringe. 'There's just the cocks in aviaries number forty-seven and forty-nine to do. Be a good chap and give them a stab, half of the stuff in each of them.'

Ten minutes later he walked into the house with a worried expression on his face.

'I am very sorry, but the plunger slipped. All that vas left has gone into the bird in pen number twelve.'

'Number twelve?! I've already injected him.'

'You told me you'd done number forty-seven and forty-nine.'

We could hardly drain the fluid out of the bird which, including the earlier dose, had now had four times the quantity prescribed for a creature weighing only one kilo.

It was with some trepidation that we approached this aviary at feed time the following morning. To say that the bird was alive and kicking was putting it mildly. He was rushing around the pen like a sex maniac released from a padded cell, while his little brown mate was clearly on the verge of collapse. We hastily cut some Christmas trees and piled them in the corners of the aviary for shelter. Thankful for this respite, she disappeared behind the branches for the rest of the day. The next morning she was still there, cowering on the sanded floor, bill open and panting for a drink. When we lifted the conifers, she raced off to the water-bowl, but she hardly had time to slake her thirst before he was up and at her.

'I theenk,' said Cees, 'I haf given him a bit too much.'

It was the understatement of the year. The cock's assaults on his wife became so vicious that we had to insert sixteen navy blue stitches into her scalp and the pair had to be separated for the rest of the breeding season. Even then our lascivious male did his best to rape the female of another species through the wire netting. We hatched no Edwards's chicks that year.

She was not the only casualty for which we were directly or indirectly responsible. In the adjoining range of pheasant aviaries resided a pair of Sonnerat's junglefowl. Not dissimilar to the red junglefowl, which is accredited with being the progenitor of all the many breeds of domestic poultry, the males of this species have been seriously persecuted in the wild, for their neck hackles are much prized for salmon and trout flies.

Our own cock, while always behaving admirably towards his three brides, took an instant dislike to my own wife. Whenever Didy took on the feeding and watering, this bird would do his best to jump onto the bucket or watering-can and dig his ferocious spurs into her arm. One such attack caused his undoing. Didy was dispensing a bucketful of windfall apples and, having successfully tipped over all the contents into his aviary, the junglefowl found his leg trapped between the handle and the pail. Struggling to free himself, he broke his leg.

Fortunately it was a clean break and we had no trouble in setting the bone and enmeshing the limb in plaster of Paris. For three weeks he was a very chastened and subdued bird and the weight of the plaster was obviously a severe encumbrance to him. When it was removed he was a changed character. Never again was Didy attacked and, to crown our veterinary accomplishment, he became the father of an entirely new mutation, now officially recognized as the lavender Sonnerat's junglefowl.

Another pheasant that is seriously inbred in captivity and may conceivably be extinct in its native China is the brown eared pheasant, first cousin of the blue eared pheasant, with which our hormone injections had been so successful. They do not have brown ears, as the name might imply, but elongated white ear coverts that form tufts of rather stiff feathers on either side of the head. Their plumage, predominantly brown, is identical in both sexes.

One common behavioural characteristic of inbreeding is that boy and girl, while existing perfectly happily together, will make little or no effort to procreate their kind. Their relationship will be platonic and unproductive. Such situations are not easy to resolve, but during the spring of 1976 we decided to attempt to breed these birds by artificial insemination.

It was a technique with which, so far as we could discover, only the Japanese had had any success. With domestic turkeys, however, it has for a number of years been the standard method of fertilization and, more recently, research in this field has been extended to chickens. The possibilities of using AI on certain breeds of exotic pheasants seemed to be worth exploring.

It so happened that a friend of ours, a veterinary surgeon at Cambridge University, knew a Huntingdonshire farmer who had studied AI of turkeys at Cornell University and subsequently introduced this technique into this country. Most generously, they both offered to give us any help and advice that they could.

On a cold and blustery day in March they first came over to the farm. The huge elms, many of them brittle with disease, creaked and groaned in the easterly wind and the daffodils bowed their heads to winter's belated onslaught. Hopalong and two of his grandsons had been selected as guinea-pigs and had been segregated in a spare pheasant aviary for the previous forty-eight hours. The first of the two younger roosters, loudly protesting that his virility should be thus put on trial, was scooped up by Cees with the landing net and brought to the foodshed, where the team of three set to work. My job was to hold the bird in a way that caused it minimum discomfort, while presenting the manipulator

123

with its appropriate organs held at a convenient height. While Norman started gently to massage the area around the cloaca and the bird's back, where the testes are found, Douglas, the vet, stood by ready to catch the ejaculate. For this he had a glass pipette, attached to a short length of clear alkathene tubing, the end of which was held between his lips.

The startled expression on the chicken's face was soon replaced by one of unconcealed, sensual pleasure. As deft fingers worked their way over his most erotic areas, there was a noticeable tensing of his body and his comb and wattles flushed a deep crimson.

'Ooh, I theenk he ees going to have an organism,' announced Cees, who by then was almost as excited as the cockerel.

'It's not exactly an organism,' laughed Douglas, 'but I think we know what you mean. Hey, mind out!' he shouted, pushing Cees's bearded face out of the way just in time to position the pipette. About three drops of cream-coloured liquid were trapped.

For Cees it was a terrible anticlimax. 'Ooh, it is such a leetle bit. I thought maybe it would . . .' and he cast his eyes towards the low ceiling of the foodshed with obvious disappointment.

At that moment his beautiful Dutch wife walked in. We were by then all tittering like schoolboys and only the cockerel seemed unamused.

'Hedy,' I said, 'You're just in time. Douglas and Norman are very kindly going to give us two or three lessons and then you, Cees and I have got to manage on our own. Now, how about your learning the suck-and-blow technique?'

After ten years at Daws Hall Wildfowl Farm Hedy was not easily shocked. Author, journalist, mannequin, *cordon bleu* cook, puppeteer, ventriloquist – she had not only turned her hand to all of these with marked success, but also somehow found time to bring up a family and dispense gargantuan meals to her husband.

'Sounds an interesting new diversion,' she said, sweeping

fine tresses of honey-blonde hair back from her face. 'Where do I start?'

'We've got the first sample,' Douglas explained, 'and we'll now try and show you how to inseminate one of the chickens.'

Cees again went off with the net and this time returned with one of the silkies from the hen house. Norman eased his hands round the bird's backside and slowly increased the pressure. What at first had appeared as a small orifice gradually opened to reveal wrinkled, pink flesh, the size of a nutmeg.

'There,' said Norman, pointing to a tiny aperture, 'That's the oviduct. Push the pipette in gently, then blow.'

It all seemed remarkably easy, but when we turned to the eared pheasants, the difficulties were soon apparent. Catching the birds, as always, was an anxiety and more than once we thought we were going to lose a bird from sheer stress of handling. The reaction was negative with the first three that we caught. Only the fourth gave a positive reaction and appeared to be enjoying himself, but even he declined to contribute anything to the pipette. In fact, this was not entirely surprising, since it was still three or four weeks before the females were due to lay and presumably the cock birds were not yet in rut. When we turned our attention to the Edwards's, a species that invariably lays early in the year, the results were only marginally more encouraging. One of the four cocks gave a positive reaction and a minute quantity of semen was obtained. Not one of the hens 'cracked', so nothing further could be done. All the brown eared pheasants, however, were segregated in separate aviaries, ready for the experiments to continue.

When the two experts returned a fortnight later, the birds were beginning to respond to the warmer weather and lengthening hours of daylight. Throughout the farm, vociferous and animated displays were greeting the arrival of spring. Lighting, of course, is a vital factor in the reproductive cycle of all birds and animals. It stimulates the

125

pituitary, a small gland lying at the base of the brain, which in turn raises the blood pressure and rouses other glands that are responsible for sexual development. Battery hens, kept in conditions of extended artificial lighting, react by laying an unnaturally large number of eggs. Conversely, underaction of the pituitary glands of veal calves, kept in almost total darkness, induces abnormal growth rates.

This time the results were a little more encouraging. The three of us watched carefully as one Edwards's hen and one eared pheasant hen were artificially inseminated and, in spare moments, we experimented ourselves with the poultry. After two more visits we were left to our own devices. Cees assumed the job of handler, Hedy stood by with pipette and tubing, while I had the responsibility of endeavouring to milk the males and crack the females.

The first cock bird that we caught seemed singularly dis-enchanted by my attempts at manipulation. We returned it to its pen and tried another. This time *succès fou* and even Cees seemed satisfied with the quantity of semen obtained. With Hedy guarding the pipette like the crown jewels Cees went off to select a suitable recipient. One brown eared hen had been squatting for us for several days – a sure sign of readiness to mate – and it was this bird that he caught. At first there was no response to my attempts to crack her and unwittingly I applied too much pressure. When I paused to reassess the situation, I saw that the force from my hands had abraded her thighs. An obviously painful area of pink flesh was exposed.

'Ven you make love to ladies,' said Cees, sucking expan-sively on his metal-stemmed pipe, 'You must be gentle. They like tender fondling and caresses, not brute force,' and he delicately massaged the back of his wife's neck, to demon-strate his technique.

'I see,' I said, feeling thoroughly inadequate, and tried a different approach to my long-suffering *amoureuse*.

To my delight, she immediately responded by disclosing her most intimate regions. Hedy inserted the pipette and

126

quickly blew down the tube. The bird laid the following evening and twenty seven days later a rufous brown chick emerged from the egg. Altogether, during that year, a total of five young pheasants were born from artificial insemination. These results, while by no means spectacular, added a new dimension to the possibilities of preserving endangered species for future generations to enjoy.

1976, in more ways than this, proved an eventful year for all of us. One of the leading galleries in London agreed to put on, the following year, a one-man exhibition of Tim's paintings and etchings. Didy was invited to San Diego, and then on to Mexico, to lecture on our methods of keeping rare and exotic pheasants. And Cees flew off to the Himalayas.

The small, partridge-like, blood pheasant is a bird that for many years had defied all attempts by aviculturists to keep and breed it in captivity. It was, as much as anything else, the seeming impossibility of keeping these birds alive and happy in the western world that had induced me to make, in 1970, two separate expeditions to Nepal and India to collect breeding birds. For five of the six subsequent years we had been fortunate enough to rear offspring from these and to carry out research on their very specialized requirements. Then, in the summer of 1976, a friend of our's in Nepal wrote to say that the government there had agreed to issue a collecting permit for up to twenty blood pheasants. It was too good an opportunity to miss. At last there was a chance of establishing, through these birds and the small stock that currently existed in aviaries in France, England and the States, a self-sustaining reserve of these elusive members of the pheasant family.

The blood pheasant is not currently considered to be endangered in the wild, but its steep and forbidding homeland in the high Himalayas is such that few foreigners have been privileged to observe it and little is known of its feral status. In a period of four weeks, specifically searching for these birds, I myself had seen only two coveys. Valuable, therefore, as the collecting licence was, it bore little relationship to ten

127

pairs of blood pheasants, safely ensconced in their aviaries on the farm. A suitable trapping area had to be reconnoitred in advance; at least one person had to travel there from England; arrangements for Sherpas and trekking equipment had to be made; special travelling boxes, to allow for feeding and watering, had to be constructed; an incalculable number of oriental officials, from Delhi onwards, had to put their rubber stamps on an incalculable number of abstruse documents; and, above all, the birds had to be caught, housed in some form of makeshift aviary at around 12,000 ft, induced to feed, and then brought down safely to Kathmandu before being flown to this country. Didy and I decided that there was only one person we knew who could possibly fulfil all these requirements. Cees was booked to fly to Nepal at the end of October.

It was the preparatory arrangements that caused him some of his biggest problems. First, he had to summon up the courage to bare his arm for the necessary injections and innoculations. For a whole week he hovered round the farm with a lugubrious and fatalistic expression on his face, convinced that the doctor would pierce some vital vein or artery. That operation safely over, his next concern was for the acquisition of a sleeping bag and pair of mountaineering boots of sufficient dimensions. As chance would have it, he had recently made friends with a policeman from Berkshire, who measured six foot and eleven inches, and it was from this man that he hoped to borrow these items of equipment. (The policeman, incidentally, had spent his last holidays in Scotland with a member of the force, who was no less than seven foot two). The constable's sleeping bag proved ideal, but the boots were too small, so recourse had to be made to a footwear manufacturer who, for an enormous sum, fashioned a special pair. Other items of trekking equipment were provided by our friend in Nepal, who also made all the administrative arrangements for reconnaissance of the trapping area, the hire of Sherpas and porters, transport, and veterinary and export permits.

128

The first part of his journey in Nepal posed no problem. A two and a half hour Landrover drive from Kathmandu took him, Ang Phu and two other Sherpas, to Barabhise, but thereafter Shank's pony was their only means of transport. Gradually they ascended, in a north-easterly direction, passing through magnificent forests of pine and birch, rhododendron, berberis and bamboo. After five days of strenuous walking they reached the tiny village of Beding, only two miles from the Tibetan border. The nights were excruciatingly cold. Only a few miles to the north, the peaks of Gauri Shankar and Menlungtse, both more than 23,000 feet above sea level, towered, alternately ice-blue and roseate pink on the snow-covered horizon. Having set up camp, Ang Phu directed his attentions to the search for blood pheasants. Six local trappers were engaged and Cees set about the construction of an aviary for their reception. The wire netting that had been carried by the porters from Kathmandu was unrolled and the floor of the aviary was lined with a thick layer of leaves and moss, interspersed with confier branches for cover. Stout boulders formed the walls.

For four days the trappers scoured the countryside, but of blood pheasants there was no sign. The only thing that the mist nets succeeded in catching was a yak. The nets were ruined and Cees began to despair. They moved camp, a new aviary was erected and finally, on the afternoon of the fifth day, the trappers sighted a covey of seven birds. Four were caught, but two later escaped. Nevertheless, spirits rose when the remaining pair were carried triumphantly into camp. Within two hours they were dead. In broad daylight, a marten had wriggled through the rock walls of the aviary and decapitated both of them. That evening Cees had blood pheasant soup for his supper.

The following day they moved camp once more, a new, smaller aviary, entirely of wire netting this time, was constructed and the services of six more trappers were engaged. Confidently, they told Cees that within two days they would get him thirty birds. While they were away, working the snares, Cees and Ang Phu watched ten blood pheasants drinking from the Rolwaling River below the camp. The catch that day was two cocks and a solitary hen.

The twelve trappers, who were paid purely on results, were on the point of giving up when, late in the evening, they sighted a large flock of about fifty birds. There were ten more days remaining before the helicopter would arrive to take Cees and whatever birds had been caught back to Kathmandu for his onward flight home.

At long last their efforts were rewarded and during their remaining time in the Rolwaling Valley a total of twenty-one more blood pheasants were brought in by the trappers. Plenty of moss was collected and placed in the aviary for them to feed on and, by judiciously scattering the turkey pellets and oats that he had brought out from England, the pheasants quickly became acclimatized to captivity and their diet. Only the original three had to be force-fed and just two of all the birds collected chose to die rather than take any sustenance at all. Under Cees's gentle management and handling the remainder quickly became tame, none more so than one hen with a scarlet bill that was soon feeding from his hand. Three of the females in fact were red either all over their beaks or at the pointed end, in marked contrast to the normal black colouration. This hitherto unrecorded characteristic, coupled with marked differences in the plumage of both sexes, compared with our original birds that had been collected from a separate area in Nepal, lead him to believe that what he had was perhaps a new race of the Himalayan blood pheasant.[1]

Food began to run low, for the birds as well as for Cees and the Sherpas. Extra moss was gathered for the blood pheasants, but for several days Cees had been out of bread, sugar and meat. The few remaining tea leaves were boiled again and again to extract the last essence. Rice was almost finished and religious scruples protected the only chicken in the

[1] These birds were nominate *Ithagenis c. cruentus*, while our earlier stock was of the subspecies *Ithagenis cruentus affinis*.

130

nearby village.

Then, two nights before the helicopter was due to arrive, disaster struck. Just after Cees had retired to his sleeping bag, a jungle cat tried to get into the aviary. The birds panicked, feathers flew and bedlam reigned for close on half an hour. After a sleepless night Cess crawled out of his tent to assess the damage. Several birds had been badly scalped, but fortunately there had been no deaths. With needle, cotton and disinfectant he cleansed and sewed up the torn heads, before administering drugs in their drinking water to alleviate the stress. That night he again had no sleep. Eerie noises emanated from the freezing blackness outside, but the wild cat did not return. By the middle of the following morning Cees was airborne and heading for home.

Since telegrams from Nepal can take anything up to five days and since Cees had been cut off from any form of wireless communication for more than three weeks, we, at home, had no means of knowing how he was faring. A special quarantine centre had been prepared, sterilized feeding and drinking bowls placed inside it and Hedy had driven up to London to meet the flight on which he had been booked. Even when the aircraft left Delhi, we did not know whether he was on board. 'Don't come back till you've got the birds,' had been my parting valediction, but Cees's quiet confidence had prevailed up till the moment of his departure.

'Don't vorry,' he had replied. 'The licence is for ten pairs, so ten pairs I vill bring.'

It was exactly with this amount that he landed at Heathrow. Two spare cock birds, that were still suffering from the effects of the jungle cat's visit, had been deposited with our friend in Nepal, without whose assistance this expedition would never have been possible.

With his habitual modesty, Cees acknowledged all our congratulations.

'Cees, did you have no problems at all?' I asked.

Pensively, he sucked on his pipe for a moment or two. He looked fit and bronzed, but had lost almost two stone in

131

weight. 'Vell,' he replied, with an amused twinkle in his clear blue eyes. 'There vere some things that I missed very much and I vas a leetle frightened at times.'

'Mountain sickness and running out of tobacco?' I ventured.

'No, I had no problem with either of those and my new boots were marvellous, not a single blister. There vas no loo paper, though, in the mountains and I did not know vat to do until Ang Phu explain to me that all the Sherpas use moss. Eet vas lovely and soft and I haf brought some home with me.' Delving into his rucksack he produced what must have been a Sherpa's ration for a whole year.

Laughing, Didy asked him what it was that had frightened him.

'The breetches,' he said, 'I thought they vere going to fall down.'

'Your breetches?'

'Yes, I vas frightened that I vould drown, but Ang Phu helped me by holding my hand.'

It was some time before we realized that he was referring to the narrow, log bridges with no handrail, that span many of the mountain streams.

Cees admitted to being a little frightened at times

Chapter Seven

'Man is clever enough to obliterate a species
but he has not, as yet, found a way of
re-creating one that he has destroyed.'
Gerald Durrell – *Catch me a Colobus*

The keeping of collections of unusual birds and animals is a pastime that goes back many centuries and coincides, in all probability, with the first attempts at domestication of these creatures. Pigeons are known to have been kept in captivity, in what is now Syria, as long ago as 4500 BC. Two thousand years later elephants were semi-domesticated in India. At the same period, addax, oryx, ibex and gazelles are depicted wearing collars on Egyptian tomb pictures. Around 1150 BC, in China, the Empress Tanki built a vast marble 'house of deer' and a hundred and fifty years after this the Emperor, Wen Wang, established a zoological garden that extended over no less than 1,500 acres.

Such collections are known to have existed in Greece from the end of the 8th century BC. Later, the importation to Rome of wild animals from Africa and Asia Minor became a passion of successive emperors. Massive exploitation of wildlife began to occur, and in the Games, which finally came to cost one third of the total income of the Empire, vast numbers of animal and human lives were expended. During Trajan's reign, for example, no less than eleven thousand animals died during the *venationes* (or mock hunts) held to celebrate a single victory.

After the collapse of the Roman Empire, zoos went into decline. It is known, however, that animal collections were maintained by Charlemagne in the 8th century AD, while the Roman centurions brought with them to Britain the forerunners of our present game pheasants. Special slaves, known as *masticarii* were employed to chew grain and sweet chestnuts for the poults. These young birds were regarded as particular delicacies, along with thrushes' tongues, wild honey, flamingoes and sow udders stuffed with fried baby dormice.

To our own King Henry I is attributed the first known zoo in this country. This was housed, first, at Woodstock in Oxfordshire and later moved by his great-great-grandson, Henry III, to the Tower of London, where a menagerie was maintained until 1828. The historic ravens at the Tower are successors to birds that were once part of the natural fauna of London. In the eleventh century, when the White Tower was the only building of any size on Tower Hill and sanitation was non-existant, food and refuse were thrown from the windows to these scavengers from Epping Forest. Six hundred years later, during the reign of Charles II, the ravens had become rare and shy. At about this time the legend started that if no ravens were in the Tower, the White Tower would fall and the British Empire collapse. Since that time, fresh stocks have been introduced and carefully guarded by the Yeoman Warder, who ensures that one wing on each bird is kept clipped. There they remain, to delight the visitors and infuriate the residents of the Tower, tearing up flower-beds, pecking putty from the windows and defecating over unattended motorcars.

In Europe, Philip VI had a menagerie in the Louvre in 1333, while successive members of the House of Bourbon maintained collections of exotic fauna at Versailles. In the New World, Cortez discovered a magnificent zoo in Mexico in 1519. This collection, which included mammals, reptiles and birds of prey was so large that it needed a staff of 300 keepers.

In the days of sail, a ship's captain would carry on long voyages a supply of livestock, to provide fresh meat, eggs and milk for the crew. In Captain Cook's Journals, one finds him lamenting, in the year 1768, a storm in which 'between 3 and

4 dozn of our Poultry' were washed overboard. These early sailors and naturalists were often presented with all manner of strange and marvellous creatures, many of which survived the long journey home, feeding below decks on the surplus hay and grain that had been taken on board for the consumption of livestock on the outward journey. The majority of these exotic creatures, in due course, found their way to the menageries of the nobility and other landed gentry, where a number were sketched by the wildlife artists of the day. Among these were the Indian rhinoceros and the legendary dodo from Mauritius. A somewhat quaint situation not infrequently arose where creatures were known for many years from these drawings before they were scientifically described. The cheetal deer (or Indian axis), for example, was painted in England by Jakob Bogdani some fifty years before it became officially known to science.

The advent of modern zoos can be said to have begun with the founding of the Imperial Menagerie in Vienna in 1752. In 1793, a zoological collection started to be assembled in the Jardin des Plantes in Paris and then, in 1826, the Zoological Society of London was founded, for 'the advancement of Zoology and Animal Physiology and the introduction of new and curious subjects of the Animal Kingdom.' In November of the following year tickets were issued to allow members and their friends free access to the Gardens in Regent's Park. It was not until 1847 that the public were admitted without signed tickets. Mondays and Tuesdays became visiting days, with cheap entrance fees of 6d on Mondays.

Edward Lear, for long known more as an author of limericks and nonsense verse than as an artist of great talent, began his profession by painting many of the newly arrived birds at Bruton Street and in Regent's Park and, a little later, at Lord Derby's famous menagerie at Knowsley. His early passion was for the parrots. Before his nineteenth birthday, he had completed the drawings and lithographic plates for his first two folios and his rented rooms were soon overcrowded. 'Should you come to town,' he wrote to a friend, 'I am sorry that I cannot offer you a home pro tempore . . . for unless you occupied the grate as a seat – I see no probability of your finding any rest consonant with the safety of my parrots – seeing, that of the six chairs I possess 5 are at present occupied with lithographic prints – the whole of my exalted and delightful tenement in fact overflows with them, and for the last 12 months I have so moved – thought – looked at, – and existed among parrots – that should any transmigration take place at my decease I am sure my soul would be uncomfortable in anything but that of the Psittacidae.'[1]

Until comparatively recently, little thought was given to optimum conditions of zoo design for stimulating the breeding of the inmates. When I was a child, elephant rides, feeding times for monkeys and penguins and watching solitary lions endlessly pace the narrow confines of their concrete cages were the main attractions for young and old alike. Educational posters or displays were virtually unknown. Zoos all over the world had not had the foresight, in a rapidly changing world, to see the possibility of maintaining viable breeding stocks of threatened species. Since the early part of the 17th century, more than eighty-five species of birds and at least fifty species of mammals have become extinct. The plight of the passenger pigeon is well known, yet this was a bird that bred freely in zoos. When disaster struck the wild populations in the 1890's, no special efforts were made to keep a breeding nucleus in captivity. The last known specimen, which was zoo-bred, died in the Cincinnati Zoo in 1914. By a strange coincidence, the last Carolina parakeet was lost to the world in the same month of the same year at the selfsame zoo.

Today, in all developed countries, there is a radical change of attitude. The animals, birds and reptiles, with (it must be admitted) a few unfortunate exceptions, are no longer treated as prisoners, but as guests. Captive breeding of rare and endangered species has taken on a new and vital dimension.

Lear to C. Empson, 1.x.1831

Game-birds generally can benefit from properly controlled hunting

Long before the terms 'conservation' or 'reintroduction to the wild' were ever conceived, our early ancestors were well aware of the needs of judiciously harvesting game animals in the way that farmers harvest a crop. Had they obliterated a species, it would have been they themselves who would have suffered. Primitive conservation is still practised in many parts of the world. One such example is with the eider duck in Norway and Iceland, where the production of down and eggs has long been part of the national economy. Like other waterfowl, eiders will lay second and third clutches if their earlier eggs are removed. For generations this practice has continued and the birds have become almost domesticated, frequently laying in dwelling houses and farm buildings. The first two clutches are removed for food and eiderdown, but the last is zealously guarded by the local people and allowed to hatch. Every year the birds return to the same nesting sites and this inter-relationship will doubtless continue until such time as 'civilization' stretches its destructive talons into these hitherto unspoilt polar regions.

A similar pattern of interdependence was achieved with the harvesting of antelopes and other game animals as carried out by primitive tribes in Africa since time immemorial. Only the advent of Arabs and white men, with sophisticated modern weapons and an obsession for trophies, disturbed the balance of nature.

An ecological balance will only be maintained, so long as the pressures on a species in a given area are such as it is biologically able to withstand. In certain countries game-birds have directly benefited from controlled hunting, and through the finance and research put into them by sportsmen and sporting organizations. This criterion is well known and understood by most country folk. Only wayward sentimentalists and political agitators fail to appreciate the very real contribution to conservation that is made by the majority of sportsmen and landowners in this country.

Many lovers of waterfowl will have visited Slimbridge, home of the Wildfowl Trust, which was established by Sir

139

Peter Scott shortly after the last war and now attracts some two hundred thousand visitors every year. There, as at some

Every year the eider ducks return to the same nesting sites

of the major zoos, a resident staff of scientists is employed. The Trust's achievements in the fields of education, conservation and research are immense, while its collection of waterfowl is the most comprehensive ever established.

Had it not been for many happy visits that I myself paid to Slimbridge, Daws Hall Wildfowl Farm would never have come about and the same, I feel sure, applies to many other private collections. One delightful aspect of our somewhat unusual profession is the willing help and advice that is invariably forthcoming from others with similar interests. During our own first waterfowl breeding season, I was on the telephone interminably to kind friends and acquaintances, who always went to great pains to give me the benefit of their experience. Now, the roles seem to be reversed, though I am only too well aware that my own limited experience does not match that of many of the people who helped me when I began; and we still visit other collections at home and overseas, at every available opportunity, to discuss our problems with fellow sufferers. Anyone wishing to start a collection is well advised to do the same. There is always something to be learned, even if it is how *not* to do a particular job!

While the conservation of the two hundred and forty-seven species of swans, geese and ducks has been in good hands since 1946, the same could not have been said for certain other threatened species. Such was the case with pheasants and their close relations, which together make up the scientific order *Galliformes*.

For a number of years, however, a number of our friends had been conscious of this fact and it was, accordingly, for the conservation of species like the Edwards's, blood and brown eared pheasants that the World Pheasant Association was founded in 1975.

In June that year an unlikely group of people had assembled at the Royal School of Medicine in London to discuss the possibilities of forming such an organization. Among others, there was a landowner, a banker, a kidney surgeon, a civil engineer, a country doctor, a game farmer, a Scots hotelier, the retired director of a well-known tobacco company and the manufacturer of the blue cardboard that goes round a famous brand of battery. Not one of us was a scientist, but all of us had in varying ways – through bird-watching, shooting or the keeping of captive collections – had many hours of pleasure from pheasants, grouse and other game-birds. Aware of the problems that faced many such birds in the countries of Asia and elsewhere, this heterogeneous band vowed to make a practical contribution to their conservation.

To begin with, the World Pheasant Association had no funds, no governing body, no members and no rules – nothing, in fact, but a title and a determination to succeed.

Three months after we met in London an inaugural meeting was held at the home of one of our founder members. We had no idea whether two people or two hundred would turn up. In fact, the attendance was well into three figures and within a year the membership had topped five hundred.

Daws Hall became the first proper headquarters of the organization, thus enabling us to meet people from all over the world with similar interests and aims. I stress the word 'proper', for in fact our very first headquarters was on the banks of the Helmsdale. Shortly after the inaugural meeting, Didy and I took a brief, but badly needed holiday, fishing in the north of Scotland. While each of us took it in turn to wield a salmon rod, the other, assisted by a much amused ghillie, struggled to compile the list of members and compose the first newsletter.

Later that year Didy flew to the States to attend a bird convention and to publicise the aims and advantages of membership of our new association. There she found a minor, unforeseen problem. WPA, in the United States, stands for Work Projects Administration, the equivalent of being 'on the dole'. The convention was held at Reno, Nevada – a smaller version of Las Vegas – where divorces were advertised at $17.50. It was an unlikely spot for such a convention, though Didy reported that there was a galaxy of extremely gaudy birds of the unfeathered variety in evidence. Her visit and subsequent exchanges led to the forging of strong ties of friendship with like-minded people from across the Atlantic, and international projects were soon being planned. Important new arrivals to the fold included a manufacturer of moulds for plastic dolls and the inventor of a machine that spewed out no less than two hundred custard pies every minute.

At the time of writing, only two years from its formation, WPA has a membership embracing peoples of more than forty different nations. Every day, Charlie, our village postman, staggers into the house with bundles of mail from all over the world. In our office, puppies and orphaned ducklings add their own brand of foreign postmark, as Didy struggles with the chaos. Between Cees, ourselves and various friends we can cope with a surprising number of European languages, but a recent letter from a member in

142

Japan caused problems. Our correspondent, who had clearly done a lot of work with his English dictionary, wrote that he needed our help 'to posterior my white precious metals'. It transpired that he was referring to the rearing of his silver pheasants.

Administering the headquarters of WPA has been a hectic but edifying experience. Soon, however, a more permanent base, with salaried staff, may have to be found, for the tasks facing the association are immense and many abler hands than ours must play their part.

The conservation of wild places and wildlife is becoming increasingly important and time seems to be a permanent enemy. With any diminishing species, the foremost consideration should be to establish why it has been reduced to such a parlous state. With pheasants, the prime causes are generally habitat destruction and illegal hunting. To the hill tribes living in India or Pakistan, the cheer pheasant and Western tragopan are regarded as no more than food for hungry stomachs. The indigenous forests are considered merely as a source of firewood or, worse still, browsing areas for hordes of ubiquitous and destructive goats.

The removal of threatened forms of wildlife to safer areas is one of several measures that can be taken, and the importance of aviculture to conservation is self-evident. However, the importation of wild stock, unless carried out in a skilled and responsible manner, can itself give rise to a new hazard. All rare objects have a price. The creation of a market for endangered creatures will, without strictly applied controls, accordingly impose an additional threat to their survival. It has already happened with butterflies in Taiwan and New Guinea, ivory in Africa and tiger skins in Asia.

No organization can attempt to carry out a programme without, first and foremost, a dedicated membership and, secondly, sufficient funds. Shortly after its inception WPA launched an international appeal and, as a result of a most heartening response, a large number of projects have already been initiated, and many more are in the pipeline. Cees's

143

expedition to Nepal to collect blood pheasants, and research on artificial insemination of gamebirds were but two of the earlier projects.

The AI experiments, which began in a lighthearted fashion on this farm in 1976, were extended last year to Cambridge University, where a group of brown eared pheasants, loaned by members of WPA, were kept in small, individual pens throughout the breeding season and all matings were conducted by scientists using this technique. Fertility among the first hundred eggs laid was close on 75 per cent. All of the cock birds, some of which had never fertilized their hens under normal aviary conditions, were shown to be capable of producing viable semen; and this after more than a hundred years of close inbreeding. A short term solution has thus been found, but more research is now needed on the remedies for abnormal breeding behaviour of captive birds. To this end, experiments conducted by small private breeders can contribute greatly to our knowledge of these wonderful birds.

The Edwards's pheasant, now possibly extinct in its native Vietnam and certainly inbred in captivity, is also receiving maximum attention. The father of young Philip, owner of Fuzzy's sexually recalcitrant mate and another founder member of WPA, is now the official stud book holder for this species. Through his records he can advise pheasant breeders all over the world on the best possible pairings to obviate infertility or genetic degenerations. (And before leaving Fuzzy, I should perhaps add that she herself may be a future candidate for AI, since this has already been carried out with marked success with peregrine falcons, bald eagles and other birds of prey.)

Field research on the status and ecological requirements of many gamebirds has also got under way and valuable data are being assembled. Students from India, Pakistan and Thailand have already attended training courses in England, and scientists, in these and other countries, are now studying rare or threatened species in their dwindling

144

natural habitats. No international conservation movement can afford to ignore the interests of local people, particularly in the developing countries. It has been a tribute to the early membership of WPA that many aviculturists in this country have loaned breeding pairs of endangered pheasants to the Association so that a supply of eggs can be flown to Pakistan and elsewhere. Many of these have been hatched and the progeny successfully reared and administered by local wild-life organizations, for eventual release into the wild under the right conditions.

Education of all people into the need for preserving their wildlife for posterity is of the utmost importance. It is a slow and difficult task and one should, I believe, focus one's attention on the younger generations. A pilot project of the World Pheasant Association has been to arrange for educational posters, describing the habits and status of the six Nepalese pheasants and printed in the vernacular, to be distributed to every village and school within that kingdom. Each poster contains a message from the King, urging his subjects to preserve what is part of their natural heritage. Similar projects in other countries will follow as funds permit.

In the developing countries of Asia and elsewhere, there is a nucleus of men and women who realize the value of conserving their gamebirds. WPA has been fortunate in gaining the support and co-operation of many such individuals and organizations. Without this, our task would be impossible. Already one third of the world's pheasants are endangered. Other groups of birds within the scope of the Association, for instance the curassows and guans of Middle and South America, are currently in an even worse plight. The extent of the challenge is daunting, and we can only hope that the flame which we and others have kindled will be kept alight for many years after we are gone.

145

Appendix One

Starting a collection

The following notes, it should be stressed, are in no way intended as an avicultural manual. They combine the general principles of aviculture of waterfowl and pheasants with a few personal observations learned from my fifteen years of experience with these birds. Anyone wishing to start a collection is well advised to visit as many existing collections as possible and to acquire suitable literature on the subject. Both the Wildfowl Trust and the World Pheasant Association list a number of collections that are open to their members, and recommended books can also be obtained by members from these two organizations.

The three golden rules for starting a collection are:

1. *Ensure your birds are adequately protected*
I make it a principle never to sell birds to people without asking them what measures they are taking for their protection. All too frequently I receive the reply, 'Oh, my cat never kills any birds,' or 'Well, I've got an island . . .' These people leave our farm empty-handed.

Birds that are pinioned are extremely vulnerable to predators and it is unfair to the birds to keep them unprotected. While domestic waterfowl respond rapidly to being driven into some form of housing at night, the wild or ornamental breeds should not (and often cannot) be subjected to this treatment.

In most parts of Britain protection is essential against

foxes, dogs, cats, stoats, rats and weasels. Only the smallest of wire netting (one inch mesh or less) will exclude the last three, and for most people this type of wire will be so expensive as to preclude its use. Stoats, weasels and rats must consequently be controlled by trapping and poisoning *within* the main enclosure.

To prevent predators such as foxes from burrowing, climbing or jumping into waterfowl pens, the wire netting should be buried and an overhang constructed at the top, as shown diagrammatically on the page opposite.

Posts can be either angle-iron stakes or creosoted hardwood. Since the total width of wire required, including the two folded sections, is nine foot, it is advisable to buy different gauges for the two halves and join them at the centre straining wire. For the top half, a lighter and cheaper gauge wire of three inch mesh will suffice, while for the bottom half, wire of the most durable small mesh (two inches maximum) that one can afford should be used. *All* wire netting should be liberally coated with a tar or bitumen based solution, best applied after erection with a paint roller. Wire treated like this every four or five years will not only lose much of its hideousness, but will long outlive its owner.

Other vermin that if possible should be excluded are moorhens, which harrass small ducks and kill their young, and winged predators, like crows and magpies, which will steal their eggs.

If the waterfowl are to be segregated in separate enclosures within the perimeter fence, a fence of three foot height will retain all pinioned birds.

Pheasants are best confined to covered aviaries. If these are built within the main enclosure, no extra protection is required. Otherwise, the perimeter wire of the aviaries needs to be buried to avoid vermin tunnelling their way in. Pheasant aviaries ideally should be of sufficiently small gauge wire to exclude not only rats, but sparrows and starlings, which are potential disease carriers and robbers of expensive food.

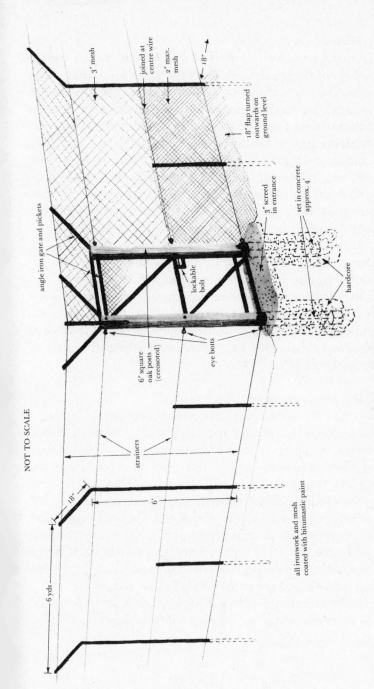

NOT TO SCALE

3" mesh

joined at
centre wire

2" max.
mesh

18"

18" flap turned
outwards on
ground level

3" screed
in entrance

set in concrete
approx. 4'

hardcore

angle iron gate and pickets

lockable
bolt

6" square
oak posts
(creosoted)

eye bolts

strainers

18"

6'

6 yds

all ironwork and mesh
coated with bitumastic paint

Fig. 1 *Construction of perimeter fences*

2. Make certain you buy good stock

To many amateurs all birds of a particular species tend to look the same, but anyone with experience will quickly learn to detect birds that are old, ill, badly pinioned or impure (i.e. hybrids). By establishing contact with the owners of other collections, you will be able to learn of reliable sources for obtaining sound, healthy stock. Always try to buy young, hand-reared birds and beware of advertisements for 'breeding pairs'. These are often being sold because they are of no further use to their present owners. Whenever possible buy unrelated stock, best achieved by getting males from one source and females from another.

Newly acquired pheasants should always be wormed on arrival and given, in their drinking water, a multi-vitamin additive to obviate the stress of movement.

Breeds of waterfowl that are known to be aggressive – South American geese, Canada geese, shelduck, cereopsis, and others – all should ideally be provided with individual pens, and should not be taken on unless segregated quarters are available.

3. Don't run before you can walk

It is very tempting, particularly if you can afford them, to rush off and buy hooded mergansers, buffleheads, peacock pheasants and other gems of the avian world – Don't. Prices for different breeds vary, not only according to their rarity, but also on how easy they are to keep and breed. Many of the most colourful ducks (mandarins, Carolinas, red-crested pochard, etc.) are, happily, very low in the price range, and the same applies to ornamental pheasants. It is with these and similar birds that the beginner is advised to start. When these varieties have been kept and bred successfully – birds that fail to breed are either poor stock or getting the wrong treatment somewhere along the line – then is the time gradually to try one's hand with the more difficult species.

Appendix Two

The management of ornamental waterfowl

WATER

Almost no pond is too small for a pair of exotic ducks or geese. Surprisingly, the areas that pose more problems are large lakes, for, unless the owner has unlimited funds, both the adequate protection and the acquisition of sufficient stock is far from easy. Half a dozen pairs of rare waterfowl can be easily lost in acres of beautiful water and reed-beds!

Rivers, too, are not ideal, unless a sympathetic local water authority allows bank to bank fencing. A series of natural ponds, preferably with running water and a minimum depth in all seasons of two foot, is probably best of all. Diving ducks, however, should not be kept in very shallow water; and there are many breeders who have excellent results with birds kept on concrete-lined ponds. Waterfowl are not good gardeners and will quickly destroy water lilies and similar plants.

SHELTER

No shelter, apart from natural shrubs and wind-breaks, is required, except for a few of the more delicate breeds. Tropical species are susceptible to frostbite in very severe weather and are not recommended for the beginner, as heated, indoor accommodation should be available. Diving ducks (e.g. pochard and tufted) will remain on the water at night and, by moving around, will keep open a small area when temperatures drop below freezing. For this reason at least one pair should be included in every collection.

The larger the area of water and land that is available, the more natural food that will be found by the birds. This can include worms, various forms of aquatic life, acorns, wild seeds and grass. Apart from this, all penned waterfowl require at least one daily feed and preferably two. The principle of nutrition is to give a high protein ration just before and during the breeding season (March to the end of June in the northern hemisphere) and a lower protein 'maintenance' ration during the rest of the year. This can be achieved as follows:

	Maintenance Period	*Breeding Period*
1st feed	Turkey growers pellets	Turkey master breeders pellets
2nd feed	Wheat, barley or oats	Turkey master breeders pellets

Geese live predominantly on grass and one pair requires an area of approximately 300 square yards. Swans, too, feed on grass and aquatic vegetation and should not be kept on small, artificial ponds.

Waterfowl that exist mainly on live animal/insect foods in the wild (e.g. eiders, goldeneye and mergansers) will benefit from a higher protein ration. This can be provided in the form of dog biscuits or brown bread, thrown to them in the water.

In a mixed collection, the feed should be distributed in a variety of regular places – pelleted food on the dry land and cereals in shallow water – to ensure that all the stock can eat the required amount. Beginners almost invariably overfeed. A suitable quantity is that which the birds will consume in approximately fifteen minutes. Waste food will encourage rats and other vermin.

During the breeding season, however, there are positive advantages in providing the birds with a permanent supply of pellets, *so long as* protection against sparrows, etc. can be

solid roofing

Fig. 2 *Modified feed hopper for adult waterfowl*

ensured. Conventional feed hoppers are not sparrowproof, but the design shown above has proved very effective on this farm:

NESTING

The best nesting cover is what nature itself provides – reeds, long grass, bushes, shrubs and hedgerows. Certain species, notably mandarins, Carolinas and goldeneye, nest in hollow trees in the wild. These birds, when pinioned, should be given elevated nesting areas, either in the form of hollow logs, baskets or boxes, best positioned above the water. Other artificial nesting contraptions include milk churns, wooden beer barrels and piles of brushwood.

Waterfowl generally nest in the spring and early summer. Clutches vary between species and average from four to a dozen eggs. If the first clutches are removed for artificial incubation, the birds will normally lay a second, and even third, clutch. Eggs should be stored, pointed end downwards in an egg-tray or on sand, in a cool place. Geese and swans are excellent parents, but ducks are notoriously bad. The hatching and rearing of their offspring is best confined to broody hens and bantams, or to totally artificial means – incubators and electric/gas rearing equipment, such as are used on commercial game farms.

Fig. 3 *Recommended artificial nesting areas*

HATCHING

Both broodies and incubators need careful siting. For the latter a stone or concrete building with good air flow and a constant temperature of 60°–70°F is recommended. There are all manner of machines on the market and the beginner is best advised, after working out his budget, to follow the recommendations of breeders who have had experience with a variety of incubators and hatchers in the appropriate price range. Having made his selection, he must follow the manufacturer's instructions meticulously, particularly with regard to temperature, wet bulb reading and sterilization.

For most hobbyists, broody hens or bantams are ideal for hatching and are as near to nature as one can get. The old gamekeepers' method of siting broody boxes out of doors in a shady position, on well drained soil, is very effective. The

154

hens are let off their eggs once a day and tethered by one leg, for feeding, drinking and defecation.

Fig. 4 *Daily exercising of broody hens*

At Daws Hall Wildfowl Farm, the broody boxes are sited in a cool, covered shed, on a brick-surrounded pit of peat. Mouse-proof wire netting is stapled to the bottoms of the boxes, the pit is saturated with water at the start to each breeding season, clean barley straw is used to line each nest and a homemade, electric 'candler' is situated within easy reach of all the eggs. When the broodies are lifted off each afternoon, they are placed in nearby cages for their 10–15 minute break.

Potential broodies are best selected in the evening, when they will be found sitting tightly on their nests, rather than going to roost. They should then be lifted, dusted with pyrethrum-based, anti-parasitic powder and transferred to a clutch of wooden or chicken eggs in a broody box. Only when they have properly settled on these should they be given the intended clutch of eggs to incubate.

The first candling should take place after seven days,

Fig. 5 *Daws Hall broody shed*

when the growing embryo can be clearly seen in all fertile eggs. The remainder can at this stage be discarded. Thereafter, candling should take place at least weekly, to check on development, and all addled or broken eggs must be removed.

The candler is the only effective method of gauging, through examination of the air cell, whether or not the humidity level is correct. Air cells that are too large mean

Fig. 6 *Candler*

insufficient humidity and vice versa. With incubators, this can be rectified by increasing/decreasing the water

156

in the machine. Broodies, in this respect, are much more reliable than incubators and eggs set under them are seldom if ever too damp. Where, however, they are too dry, and particularly during the last 48 hours before chipping, a little warm water can be sprinkled or sprayed over the clutch when the hen is off the nest.

As soon as the eggs start to chip the hen should be left undisturbed, without food or water, until the entire clutch is hatched and dry. This normally takes forty-eight hours.

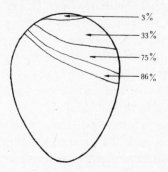

Fig. 7 *Development of the air cell in relation to percentage incubation age*

REARING WATERFOWL

Young birds hatched by a broody can be moved with their foster parent to a coop and run, or similar accommodation out of doors, providing that there is some form of shelter and protection against vermin. For many years we have used brooders developed by the Wildfowl Trust, of which full specifications can be found in the Trust's *Seventeenth Annual Report, 1964–65*. These are so designed as to be usable either for broody hens, or infra-red heating lamps. We have also reared thousands of waterfowl, without broodies, starting them in small indoor pheasant rearing pens, on sand and under lamps (see Fig. 11 page 168), and then moving them, at about three weeks of age, to the Wildfowl Trust brooders outside. After three weeks in these, without any heat, they should need no housing whatever. It is only at this stage that we allow them to swim in specially constructed, nursery pools.

The standard feed for young waterfowl up to 4–6 weeks of age is a proprietory brand of starter crumbs. To encourage them to eat what to them is an entirely unnatural food, we sprinkle a little minced, hard-boiled egg on top of the crumbs. Also to be advocated, when there is no broody hen, is the transferring of a slightly older duckling to each new brood, and this bird should quickly teach the others to feed. It is noticeable that the newly-born chicks are attracted by certain colours, noticeably yellow – hence the hard-boiled egg – and red. Another ingenious idea, that I learned from a friend is to put children's Smarties (brightly coloured, sugar-coated choc drops) on top of the crumbs. The ducklings will frantically pursue the red and yellow ones round the bowl, inadvertently taking in the crumbs in the process!

If heating lamps are used, the temperature should be maintained at around 90°F for the first three days. The lamp can then be gradually raised, depending on the weather, so that no heat whatever is necessary when the birds are 2 – 3 weeks old. Young ducklings grow remarkably quickly and are usually fully grown and feathered by the time they reach two months. Growers or rearing pellets should be introduced in place of crumbs when the birds are 4–6 weeks old, There-after their diet should to all intents and purposes be as for adults.

Surprisingly perhaps, newly born waterfowl that are hatched artificially do not always take kindly to a swim. For them, deep water is best avoided since without natural waterproofing at birth they can quickly become chilled. At Daws Hall Wildfowl Farm, non-swim water containers, in a variety of sizes are used for the first 2–3 weeks.

If duckweed is available, this is an excellent form of natural food, usually full of small aquatic creatures, and it will of course float on top of the water. These bowls are emptied and cleaned every morning and merely kept topped up during the day. When not fresh, enteritis can develop.

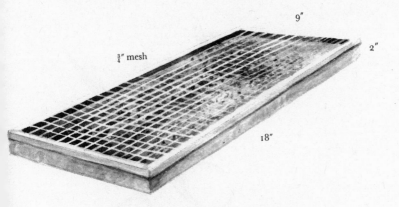

Fig. 8 *Water bowl for young birds*

Goslings and cygnets, as explained earlier, are best left to the care of their natural parents. If, however, an extra clutch is to be hoped for and the first one is hatched artificially, it is important to remember that short grass or other greenfood is essential to them at an early age. For this reason, coupled with their need for a mother figure, these birds are better entrusted to a large broody hen, rather than to an inanimate lamp.

Waterfowl are, to most people, more beautiful to watch when free-winged than when pinioned. The difficulty is to induce them to stay. For really valuable species the risk is too great to attempt, but for a few of the commoner birds it is, in my opinion, always worth a try. This can only be achieved when they are born on the place and where there is a liberal expanse of water for them to take up permanent residence. Otherwise, pinioning should be carried out during the first week of their lives. Done properly, as shown below, it is a permanent operation and the primary feathers can never grow.

RECOMMENDED BREEDS FOR THE BEGINNER

Altogether there are 247 known species of waterfowl. There are several that have never been kept in collections; others that tax to the utmost the skill and ingenuity of experts, while two species, the mallard and the black duck,

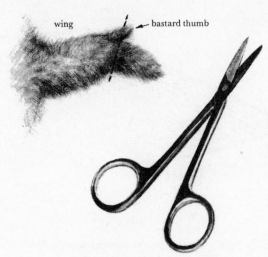

wing ← bastard thumb

Fig. 9 *Pinioning young waterfowl*

are so prolific and so greedy as to warrant their exclusion.

The beginner is best advised to keep those birds that combine maximum interest and beauty with comparatively low cost of purchase and a willingness to breed readily in captivity. To my mind, the following possess all these characteristics and are best kept in pairs.

Species	*Incubation Period (days)*
Fulvous Tree Duck	28–32
Snow Goose	24
Barnacle Goose	24
Bahama Pintail	25
Northern Pintail	26
Laysan Teal	25
European Wigeon	25
Chiloe Wigeon	25
Blue-winged Teal	24
Cinnamon Teal	24
Red-crested Pochard	26
Tufted Duck	26
Mandarin	28–30
Carolina (N. American Wood Duck)	28–32

Appendix Three

The management of ornamental pheasants

AVIARY CONSTRUCTION

With the exception of peafowl, which are best seen at liberty in a large garden or park, exotic pheasants can only be kept safely in aviaries. With careful planning and judicious planting of shrubs, these pens can enhance the beauty of the birds. Cock pheasants are often extremely vicious towards other birds of the same family, so not more than one adult pair (or one cock with several hens in the case of polygamous species) should be kept in each aviary.

The minimum aviary dimensions recommended for birds of average size (e.g. silver or Reeves's pheasants) are 15 ft long by 6 ft wide. Larger species require more room and the larger the aviary the more pleasing it is for both observer and occupant. Our own aviaries are built in blocks of between six and ten and, as can be seen below, they not only vary in length, but are larger than the minimum recommended size. All our pheasants are kept free-winged and pinioning undoubtedly spoils their appearance.

The framework for these aviaries can be of metal or wood and the overall height 6 to 8 ft. The sides and backs of the shelters can be built of overlapping planks of timber, creosoted for protection against the weather. Pheasants will always roost on the highest available perch that is provided, so these should be situated in the shelters which are covered in translucent PVC. If all predators and vermin are to be excluded, including sparrows and other wild birds coming for the feed, ¾inch netting should be used on the outside walls and roofs of the open flights. To save unnecessary

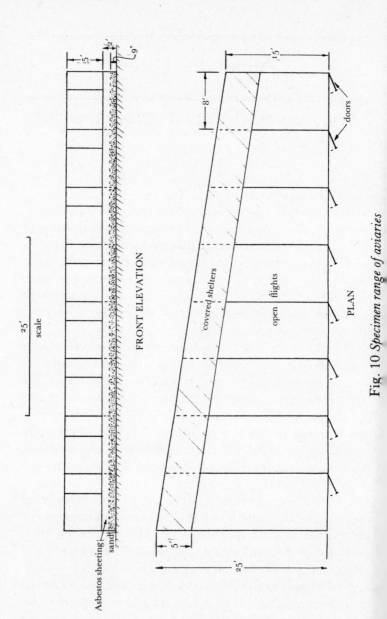

FRONT ELEVATION

Asbestos sheeting

sand

25'

scale

covered shelters

open flights

doors

PLAN

15'

8'

5'

25'

15'

2'

9"

Fig. 10 *Specimen range of aviaries*

162

expense, the dividing partitions can all be of larger (2 inch) mesh. Exclusion of all predators is strongly recommended. Not only can rats, stoats, etc. kill the birds, but they and sparrows also, are robbers of food and potential carriers of diseases.

For tropical breeds, (which are not recommended for the beginner) our aviaries are modified to include a completely enclosed shelter. When the weather is very cold, the birds are kept inside and extra warmth provided by some form of artificial heating. We have found the most effective system to be electric heating cables laid in concrete on the floors.

Pheasants, like human beings, dislike damp and draughts, so careful consideration must be given to the siting of aviaries, particularly bearing in mind the direction of the prevailing wind.

The floor of the aviary is a matter for personal preference, often depending on the location. The conventional design used extensively and successfully in many countries is one of grass. On our farm we have pioneered the use of sand, both for breeding birds and young poults, the latter were previously kept on movable pens on grass. The advantages of sanded aviaries are as follows: almost total elimination of soil-borne diseases and those carried by earthworms; strict control of food and water intake through the birds being unable to eat grass; and avoidance of mud, which pheasants detest, after heavy rain. When making a new range of aviaries, we put stout railway sleepers around the perimeter of the area first, then bring the sand in by mechanical dumper and spead it evenly to a depth of nine inches before starting construction.

Whether sand or grass is selected, evergreen shrubs (including poisonous ones which the birds will not eat) should be planted in the aviaries. These not only improve the look of the pens, but also provide essential cover and shade. Until natural cover has grown up, brushwood and evergreen branches should be placed in each pen, shortly before the nesting season, and removed after the birds have finished laying. Recommended shrubs include:

Medium and low growing conifers, particularly *Juniperus virginiana, J. x media* 'Hetzii,' *J. x media* 'Pfitzeriana', *Chamaecyparis lawsoniana* 'Tamariscifolia' and *Taxus baccata* 'Repandens'.
Snowberry (*symphoricarpos*)
Cotoneasters and berberis
Chamaecyparis lawsoniana 'Stewartii' and 'Lutea' (keep trimmed)
Hebes
Ceanothus   *Eleagnus ebbingei*
Broom   *Lonicera nitida*
All of these thrive in sandy soil, but should be planted with a bucketful of compost, peat or leafmould, and require wire netting protection against the birds until they are established.

CHOICE OF PHEASANTS
Of the 49 species, some are so rare as to be almost prohibitive in price, while others require very specialized care and attention. Listed opposite is a selection of recommended birds for the beginner and it will be noted that this includes a number of breeds that are endangered in the wild. It cannot be stressed too strongly that there is probably no other branch of aviculture where the hobbyist can make such a positive contribution towards the conservation of threatened species. All those listed are hardy and require no extra protection in cold weather.

FEEDING OF ADULT STOCK
All pheasants will respond to a well-balanced diet. Ideally, this should vary according to the season and the principles recommended for the feeding of waterfowl (Appendix II, page 152 apply equally to pheasants. The birds will also relish fruit, chopped onions, carrots, spinach and lettuce, according to season. For the best breeding results, it is important to ensure that the birds are not too fat during the maintenance

Species	Status in the wild E = Endangered NE = Not Endangered	Recommended pairings M = Monogamous P = Polygamous	Breeding age (years)	Incubation Period (days)
Sonnerat's Junglefowl	NE	P	1	21
Himalayan Monal	NE	M	2	27
Nepal Kalij	NE	P	1	25
Edwards's Pheasant	E	M	1–2	24
Swinhoe's Pheasant	E	P	1–2	25
Silver Pheasant	NE	P	1–2	25
Brown Eared Pheasant	E	M	2	27
Blue Eared Pheasant	NE	M	2	27
Cheer Pheasant	E	M	1	27
Elliot's Pheasant	E	P	1	25
Hume's Bar- tailed Pheasant	E	P	1	26
Mikado Pheasant	E	P	1–2	27
Reeves's Pheasant	NE	P	1	25
Golden Pheasant	NE	P	1–2	22
Lady Amherst Pheasant	NE	P	1–2	22

(non-breeding) period, and for this a regulated ration consisting of Turkey growers pellets in the morning and cereals in the afternoon is recommended. This is best achieved by discovering the *ad lib* intake and then feeding 80 per cent of that quantity during this time of year. A simpler, though somewhat less accurate method is to give the birds, twice daily, that amount which they will consume in 5–10 minutes. If sparrow-proof wire netting has been used in aviary construction it is quite possible to give measured weekly rations of the pellets which can be placed in a hopper under the shelter. Birds that choose to gobble up seven days' ration in one feast will come to no harm, since they will also be receiving a daily measure of cereals. We always use chipped oats, but if these are not obtainable, wheat or barley can be given in lieu.

If, however, the wire netting does not preclude small birds, then the pellets too must be distributed by hand each day. As with waterfowl, the natural tendency is always to overfeed.

During the breeding season, the cereal ration should be halved, or even eliminated, and turkey breeders pellets given on an *ad lib* basis. Insoluble grit should be provided in each pheasant aviary and waterbowls must be kept filled and scrupulously clean.

NESTING

Like waterfowl, pheasants lay in the spring and the removal of eggs encourages further clutches. These vary in size from 4–15 eggs, apart from peacock pheasants that only lay one or two eggs in each clutch. Laying occurs in the late afternoon and usually takes place in a shallow, unlined scrape in a corner of the aviary behind cover. It is best to remove each egg as soon as possible (storing them as for those of waterfowl), for cock pheasants, and hens too, on occasions, have a tendency to be egg-eaters. This habit is difficult to break, although there are a number of remedies advocated, such as filling dummy eggs with mustard or creosote. If, as is usually the case, the male is the offender, he can be driven (through a trap door) into an empty, adjoining pen on alternate days; if, however, the female is the culprit, the only safe course is literally to sit and wait (with a good book or drink!) for each egg to be laid.

HATCHING

The principle here is the same as for waterfowl, and eggs should be put under broodies or into incubators when as fresh as possible. Our eggs are all marked, on the blunt end with a felt-tip pen, to show species, aviary number and date laid. Unlike young waterfowl, pheasant chicks are often aggressive to younger or smaller birds. For this reason, therefore, and to cater for different incubation periods, we set eggs on different days and thus achieve weekly hatches of poults that can be reared together. A typical hatching programme would be:

166

Mon. 1 May – Monal, Eared pheasants┐ All these eggs should
Wed. 3 May – Silver pheasants   ├ hatch together on
Sat. 6 May – Golden pheasants   ┘ 28 May.

Embryo and air cell development are similar in all eggs
and it must be remembered that, under artificial conditions,
more eggs fail to hatch through faulty incubation than
through any other cause. The wily old broody hen, whatever
her other faults, has much to recommend her to the small
breeder.

REARING ORNAMENTAL PHEASANTS

As with waterfowl, there are basically two methods – broody
hens in coops and runs, or brooders that are artificially oper-
ated. Both have been used with good effect at Daws Hall
Wildfowl Farm, although latterly, to save time and labour
where large numbers of chicks are involved, rearing has been
done indoors under infra-red lamps. Pheasant chicks are
often very wild at birth and very susceptible to chilling. To
contain them close to the source of heat during the early
stages, boxes of rough-sawn timber are used. Corrugated
paper is placed on the floor for the first 3–4 days, to
strengthen their legs and obviate the intake of sand or other
unwanted material. (This paper is not necessary for young
waterfowl).

Turkey-starter crumbs should be given to young chicks for
the first 6 weeks. As an inducement to start feeding, hard-
boiled egg – put the whole egg, including the shell, through a
mincer – can be sprinkled on top of the crumbs. Live insects,
particularly mealworms and aphids, are also excellent in nutritional value and can be given sparingly to rare or difficult
broods. Care must be taken that chicks do not drown and, for
the first couple of days, a few pebbles in the water drinkers are
recommended.

Heating lamps should be gradually raised, according to
the weather, and we remove the special boxes and put in low
perches after the first week. The time to switch off the arti-

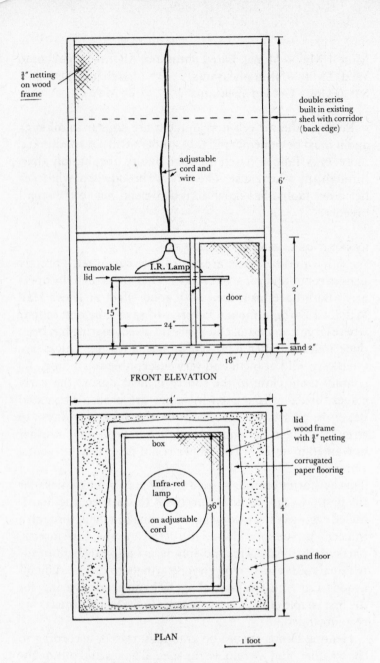

FRONT ELEVATION

¾" netting on wood frame

double series built in existing shed with corridor (back edge)

6'

adjustable cord and wire

removable lid

I.R. Lamp

door

2'

15"

24"

sand 2"

18"

PLAN

4'

lid
wood frame with ¾" netting

box

corrugated paper flooring

Infra-red lamp

on adjustable cord

36"

4'

sand floor

1 foot

Fig. 11 *Pheasant rearing pens, 1st stage*

ficial heat is when the young poults roost at night on perches away from the lamp. Unlike ducklings, no rapid move to outdoor covered pens should be made. Our poults stay indoors for at least 4 weeks and as much as 8 weeks when the nights are still cold.

Green food (chickweed, chopped lettuce, etc.) will be beneficial to all young pheasants after the first week of age and does much to relieve boredom and feather-pecking. This latter habit, which can happen at any time from 3 weeks of age, is one to which pheasant breeders must always be alert. The best remedy is the use of plastic bits[1] fitted to the nostrils, coupled with trimming the upper mandibles with a pair of nail scissors.

From the indoor brooder pens our poults are moved to covered outdoor nursery aviaries, 12ft by 3ft by 6ft high, which again have sanded floors. From 8–20 weeks they are given turkey rearers pellets and a little corn each afternoon. From that age they go into larger aviaries and are treated as adults.

DISEASES

No mention of these was made for waterfowl. Not only do they have a natural resistance to many parasites and infections, but any form of prophylactic treatment of birds kept at virtual liberty is hard to effect. Pheasants, unfortunately, are generally more prone to a variety of ailments. These, however, should not cause undue problems if sensible hygiene precautions are observed and certain drugs are administered regularly at the prescribed levels. Prevention of some of the more common complaints can be summarized as follows:

Disease	Remarks
Newcastle Disease (Fowlpest)	All poultry and pheasants require a four-monthly oral vaccination of Hitchner B1 live vaccine in the drinking water.

---

[1] Obtainable from The Game Conservancy, Fordingbridge, Hampshire.

Blackhead	Ensure that an anti-blackhead drug is incorporated in the turkey feed. Confirmed cases should be treated with Emtryl.
Coccidiosis	It is most important that starter feeds up to at least 6 weeks contain coccidiostats. Sulphur-based drugs, obtainable from all veterinary surgeons provide effective treatment if there is an outbreak of this disease.
Gape worms (*Syngamus trachea*) and other parasitic worms	Tetramisole Hydrochloride should be given in the water at prescribed intervals as a preventative measure. It is not effective against adult gapes, for which Thiabendazole or Mebendazole are both recommended. These can only be administered in the feed, and the latter will provide cover against most intestinal roundworms.

Diagnosis of ailments is far from easy, even to trained veterinarians. At the slightest sign of a sick bird, the following course of action is recommended.

(a) Catch up (with a trout net) and isolate the sick bird in a small hospital pen, after first taking a faecal swab sample. Inspect plumage for lice and fleas, and if present, dust with Pybuthrin.

(b) Put a broad-spectrum antibiotic (e.g. Furaltadone) in the drinking water.

(c) Take the sample to the local vet and follow his advice.

All birds that die should be sent to the vet for an autopsy. In this way much can be learned on disease control and medication for similar casualties in the future.